paige tate
& CO.

Published by Paige Tate & Co.

Paige Tate & Co. is an imprint of Blue Star Press

PO Box 8835, Bend, OR 97708

contact@paigetate.com

www.paigetate.com

Writing by Nikki Boyd

Photography by Christopher Shane
Cover image; pages 6, 10, 13, 14 (center), 39, 54, 57, 64, 68, 69, 72, 74, 76, 77, 86, 94, 102, 176, 187, 190, 193-194, 197-200

Photography by Katie Fiedler of Katie Charlotte Photography
Pages 1, 9, 14 (left, right), 16, 19-20, 27, 31-35, 40, 44, 50-52, 59, 61, 62, 66, 70, 71, 73, 78, 81, 82, 85, 91, 99, 100, 101, 104, 106, 108, 113, 116, 119, 120, 122-126, 129, 130, 135-139, 141, 143, 147-149, 151, 152, 159, 160, 162, 175, 183, 185, 188, 189, 202, 207-209, 211, 212, 214-217, 219

Creative Market
Photographs on pages 166, 172, 174 from Creative Market under an extended license.

Design by Amy Sly & Chris Ramirez

ISBN 978-1944515683

Printed in China

10   9   8   7   6

BEAUTIFULLY ORGANIZED

A GUIDE TO FUNCTION
AND STYLE IN YOUR HOME

NIKKI BOYD

CREATOR OF ATHOMEWITHNIKKI.COM

ACKNOWLEDGEMENTS

I would like to thank God for his love and putting me on this journey. When I thought I should work a traditional nine to five job, God confirmed for me that was not my path and that my role was to share with the world how to make home a beautiful place. He is my strength and my everything.

I would like to thank my husband, Mike, for his unconditional support and love and for being such an integral part of making our house a beautiful home. He has endless patience and willingness to do whatever my heart desires. He keeps me inspired not only as a wife and mother but as a human being.

To my mom and dad, who are my everything. No matter what I do in life, they are always present and supportive. Their love for me never wavers, and if God had allowed me to choose my parents, I would not have changed his decision one bit.

To my Irish twin, my brother. Thanks for being my first guest to all the dinner parties I hosted in my room as a child. I can only imagine the amount of Play-Doh® cakes you have eaten over the years.

To the people who have kidnapped my heart, my babies Chris, Ethan, Courtney, Savannah, Caleb, Sam, and Amelia. I only gave birth to one of them, but I love them all as if they were my children. Watching these beautiful souls grow up has been one of my greatest joys in life. They have inspired many of the systems I have implemented in our home. We have created so many memories together, and I am excited to build even more.

I would like to thank the entire Paige Tate & Co. team for their dedication to this book. Their support got me through some challenging days. A special thanks to my editor Clare, for her guidance and always making me feel at the top of her list. She did not miss a beat even as she was going through the process of planning her wedding and getting married during the writing of this book. Her dedication to the book made the process a success. To my editor Alicia, for all the late nights she spent reading my

long stories and helping me shape my words to be beautifully organized in this book. She challenged me, guided me, and worked tirelessly to bring this book to life. To Amy, who beautifully brought my vision to life in the pages of this book. She immediately connected with my style and made the process of designing the pages and illustrations of this book a fun process.

To the *At Home With Nikki* team, Jennifer, Hazel, Angela, Mike, Becky, Brooke, and Kate. I could not do all that I do to help so many people bring peace and comfort to their homes without you. You are so special to me and the best team a girl could have.

To Katie and Chris, my favorite two photographers. I have such beautiful memories of all our photo shoots of my home. Katie is not only the most amazing photographer, but a fantastic person and I was honored to have her photograph my house for the book. Chris is no longer here on earth, but he is present in this book through his photography of my home.

To my friend Toni Hammersley. We get each other, and it makes for a beautiful friendship. I am so honored that she wrote the foreword for this book and continues to be such a beautiful inspiration to me.

And to my YouTube® followers who I call my friends. The reason this book was written was because of you. You have supported me from my first video and blog post. You have added so much to my life, and we will forever be friends.

TABLE OF CONTENTS

FOREWORD

As you flip through the pages of this book, get ready to become visually and thoughtfully inspired to create a home of order. Professional organizer Nikki Boyd has a unique gift of transforming a space into a captivating work of art. She sprinkles a little bit of glam with a whole lot of functionality into every space she touches. Nikki will take you step-by-step through her organizing and cleaning process and guide you along the way. She has taken the guesswork out and will help to minimize the struggles we so often run into when getting our homes in order. Her plan is simplified and systematically laid out for you. Say goodbye to clutter and chaos and hello to a beautifully organized home. This book is a jewel, and I promise you will not want to put it down.

TONI HAMMERSLEY
A Bowl Full of Lemons
Author of *The Complete Book of Home Organization*

INTRODUCTION

When I was a little girl and I was told to clean my bedroom, I did so quickly and efficiently: I simply stuffed everything under my bed and into the closet. In other words, I am not one of those fortunate souls who was born knowing how to tidy up a space. In fact, it was not until I became an adult and left my parents' home that I grew to appreciate the importance of having a beautifully organized home.

As an adult, I have had plenty of opportunities to develop my organization skills. My husband spent his career in the United States Air Force and our family traveled and moved frequently. My work history is colorful as a result. I seized new opportunities wherever we landed. I worked in human resources and social services. I worked as a school registrar, and I worked as an art framer. The common thread through my many positions was my appreciation of organizational systems and my eye for detail.

As a military spouse, I embraced each opportunity to organize our things and create a home for our family, wherever in the world my husband, our three children, and I happened to be living. There is both skill and art in making a house a home, you see. I mastered my organizational skills through our many moves and many homes. But I also developed a passion for creating a beautiful, happy home to enjoy with family and friends. We lived in houses of all sizes, and I always strived to create a warm, enjoyable space. My experience has taught me that a beautiful, happy, organized home is obtainable no matter the size of your home or the size of your budget. It's all about the feeling of "home."

"The home should be a beautiful haven for the entire family,
a place to feel safe, happy, and relaxed."

After my husband retired from the military, we settled in a beautiful home in our beloved Charleston, South Carolina. I began to pursue my passion for creating beautifully organized spaces and opened a professional organizing firm in Summerville, South Carolina to help other people achieve beauty and organization in their own homes.

> *"It is my belief that an organized home guarantees a beautiful and fulfilling life."*

Yes, this is a bold statement! But I absolutely believe it to be true. There are so many reasons to want to create a beautiful, functional home. Perhaps you live a fast-paced life and need your home to function efficiently. Perhaps you take pride in creating a homey atmosphere, a place to make memories and to enjoy time spent with the people you care about. Perhaps you relish the idea of home as a calm, peaceful retreat from the busy outside world. Your desire for a beautiful, organized space may be rooted in one of these, in all three, or in something else altogether!

WHAT IS A BEAUTIFULLY ORGANIZED HOME?

But what exactly *is* a beautifully organized home? It's important to know that there isn't a single definition or set of traits that makes a home "beautifully organized." Unique spaces, family structures, lifestyles, and priorities mean that each person's approach to their space will also be unique. What is important is that at the end of the day, your house feels like your *home*. While "home" may look wildly different from person to person, your home should exude a feeling of warmth and positivity. A well-maintained home creates a feeling of pride; you will be eager to welcome your family and friends. Does this mean that your house must be immaculate twenty-four hours a day? Absolutely not! A perpetually immaculate home is not necessarily a beautiful home—and it's not even realistic! It *is* possible, however, to create a home that makes anyone who enters feel welcome and special, carrying a beautiful experience with them when they depart.

While creating a beautifully organized home is a worthy goal in and of itself, there are also some very practical reasons to devote time to organizing and beautifying your space:

◁ SAVE TIME ▷

When your home is not in order, it becomes easy to slide into the habit of tossing items in random places. While this might feel like a minor concern, the consequences are more significant than they might at first seem. Rather than enjoying a cup of coffee and a moment of quiet reflection at the breakfast table, you might be scrambling to find car keys or to sign a permission slip. Morning after morning, chaos reigns; this can have an adverse effect on your overall peace of mind. With simple routines and systems for organization, you will save yourself so much time and effort as you go through your daily routines.

◁ SAVE MONEY ▷

Have you ever purchased an item that you already own simply because you could not locate it in your home? This is a common experience for many people, and it is one way that clutter begins to overtake a home. Have you ever wondered how much money is sitting in your home right now in the form of things that are simply taking up space without serving a purpose? By having a place for everything (and everything in its place!) and workable systems to ensure items are returned after they are used, you can eliminate frustration, reduce the tendency to "double buy," and put money right back in your pocket—perhaps even enough money for a vacation!

◁ REDUCE STRESS AND BOOST ENERGY ▷

When your home has order, your mind, body, and spirit are free from the stress of living in disorder. With proper systems in place, you can greatly reduce common daily stressors that can affect you emotionally and steal your energy, such as deciding what to make for dinner or how to stay on top of the ever-growing laundry pile. Instead, you can devote your time and energy to more important matters.

◁ FOSTER PERSONAL GROWTH ▷

Each person has talents and hobbies to hone and cultivate, for personal enjoyment or in service to others. When your home is well-organized, you are able to focus your mind, body, and spirit in ways that foster personal growth and fulfillment. You can take an art class, cook a nutritious meal, dig in your garden, or serve those in need in your community. Life becomes more meaningful and enjoyable, and it all starts at home.

◁ EXPERIENCE HAPPINESS ▷

Imagine for a moment what it would be like to walk into the home of your dreams. You cross the threshold and glide into the entryway without tripping through a sea of shoes. You nose is tickled by the scent of fresh flowers on the table. As you walk through the rooms, you see a kitchen sink devoid of dishes and a laundry basket that holds only a few items. You make a pot of tea and relax into the sofa with a good book in hand. How can this be?

This book will help you to create a home that is beautiful and organized. You deserve this! I will introduce you to the process I use with my clients. Room-by-room, you will gain control of your belongings and implement my tried-and-true systems to help your home function with ease. You will uncover and celebrate the beauty in your home. With this dual focus on organization and beauty, you will create a warm, welcoming space for yourself and for the people you cherish.

Over the years, I have collected and created organizing techniques, home décor tricks, and tips for entertaining with grace and joy. I love to help people transform their spaces with simple and efficient systems that make home life function with ease. I relish helping others to appreciate and celebrate the beauty in their homes. And once a client is finally "at home" in their beautifully organized space, it is immensely gratifying to me to know that they can enjoy their houses with family and friends in new and profound ways.

CHAPTER ONE

WHERE TO BEGIN

A client once told me that what she most wanted was to live in a beautiful home. As we walked around her house so that I could learn more about her and her space, it was abundantly clear to me that she had already achieved her goal. This client had a great eye for design and beautiful décor. I fell in love with her open floor plan and gorgeous kitchen. However, my client wasn't able to see past the many things she had accumulated and the clutter that overwhelmed the space. All the extraneous "stuff" overshadowed an otherwise beautiful area. For example, my client had enough pantry canisters to outfit three homes, but she continually bought new containers to try to make her pantry more functional. With each purchase, she moved further from function and deeper into disorganization.

The first step was simple: I asked my client to commit to not purchasing any new items throughout our time working together. With this in mind, our first task was to declutter her space with two goals: we needed to eliminate excess and we needed to "shop" the items she already owned. Decluttering was the process of curating my client's things until she was left with what was truly useful, what she truly loved, or both. This took time, but once we concluded the decluttering process, we worked to establish workable systems and helpful techniques to create and maintain well-organized spaces. Through each step in the process, my client was increasingly able to recognize and appreciate the beauty in her own home. At the end of the project, she actually screamed with joy. She had what I call a "Dorothy" moment: just like Dorothy in *The Wizard of Oz*, my client realized that she had all that she needed to "come home" the entire time.

◇

Before you roll up your sleeves and begin cleaning out closets, let's first mentally prepare you to refresh and rejuvenate your home. The truth is, no one is *making* you do this! My guess is that you already believe that a beautifully organized home will benefit you in myriad ways. Still, it's important to start out on the right foot! What motivates you? Consider some of these ways to energize yourself and generate enthusiasm for the challenge ahead!

CREATE MOTIVATORS

Creating a beautifully organized home is not an overnight process and it's not for the faint of heart. Rather, this will be a journey that requires sustained focus and dedication. While there are many long-term benefits (as I discussed in the introduction to this book), it's helpful to think about how to motivate yourself through the process of decluttering, cleaning, organizing, and beautifying your home. You don't get a cheerleading squad, but here are some ways to create motivation:

◁ POWER WORDS ▷

Whenever I am faced with a dreaded task, I tell myself "You've got this!" These are my "power words." It's simple, but this phrase gives me a kick start on any given task. What are your power words? Write them down and post the words someplace visible—the fridge, bathroom mirror, or even your phone screen saver—to motivate yourself as you work toward home organizing success.

◁ SPARKLE TIME ▷

Your "sparkle time" is the time of day that you have the most energy. Do you wake up with the sun and embrace the day, or are you a night owl, at your best when the rest of the world is asleep? Schedule your organizing sessions during your "sparkle time" and harness your energy and creativity to devise and implement new systems to organize your home.

◁ HOST A PARTY ▷

You may need to play a little trick on yourself to ignite your motivation. Host a dinner party or invite an out-of-town friend to visit for the weekend. Give yourself a comfortable amount of time before the event and embrace your hostess obligations as the motivation to get your home in order!

◁ REWARD YOURSELF ▷

You're going to work hard, and I encourage you to reward yourself as you go! Have a bottle of wine on reserve for after a decluttering session; stop for a pedicure after you haul a carload of items to a donation center. Take time to do the things you enjoy as you work; this will help you to avoid burnout and to continue to make progress toward your goals!

CREATE FAMILY BUY-IN

◇

No matter how determined and motivated you are to organize your home, you will be fighting a losing battle if the people you live with aren't on board. It can be easier said than done to create family buy-in. However, I often recommend that clients hold a "Family Home Meeting." While these family meetings can be held on an as-needed basis, I find that the meetings are most successful when families commit to meeting weekly. The purpose of the "FHM" is to gather everyone together to discuss anything (and everything!) that involves the family and the home for the coming week. Ideally, every member of the family should be a vocal participant to make these meetings fun and engaging. The FHM is *not* a lecture or a gripe session, but rather a productive time to facilitate communication among the family. In fact, I have seen some families rotate the responsibility to "lead" the meeting each week. This is always a great success. Everyone (especially children!) feel they are valued as an important member of the family "team." Most importantly, the FHM can be a useful way to communicate expectations, to assign responsibility, and to maintain accountability—all essential to the long-term maintenance of an organized home!

Over the years, I have refined my personal approach to creating functional, lovely homes. Almost any task benefits from a process; organizing your home is no different. The following steps can be adapted and applied to every room in your home. You'll be on your way to a beautifully organized home in no time!

FIVE STEPS TO A BEAUTIFULLY ORGANIZED HOME

◇

As you begin to organize your home, you are best served by working room-to-room and tackling one space at a time. For example, in your kitchen you might work on organizing the pantry during one session and the refrigerator the next. If you attempt to work in your entire home at once, you will quickly become overwhelmed and lose focus, making it difficult to create workable systems.

FAMILY HOME MEETING AGENDA ITEMS

FAMILY SCHEDULE

Discuss family member schedules for the coming week (appointments, practices, lessons, etc.). A general family calendar helps to keep everyone on the same page.

MEAL PLANNING

Discuss meal plans for the coming week, taking family member preferences and individual schedules into account.

HOME ISSUES

Discuss any issues related to the home including maintenance concerns and distribution of housekeeping responsibilities.

SUCCESSES & STRUGGLES

Keep communication flowing in your family! Have each family member discuss one success and one struggle from the previous week.

HOME NEEDS ASSESSMENT

Create a list of needs for the week; this list can help to form your shopping list. Some things to consider: field trip money, home products, supplies for school projects, etc.

TEACHING TIME

Discuss a topic that is important to your family: current events, family traditions, or faith. You may even use this time to teach your family important life skills. (See suggested topics below.)

TEACHING TOPIC SUGGESTIONS

- How to Handle a Bully
- How to Fold a Towel
- How to Set a Table
- How to Make Change
- How to Budget
- How to Wash Clothes

- How to Be a Good Citizen
- How to Load a Dishwasher
- Fire Safety
- How to Read Labels
- How to Say "No"
- How to Wake Up On Time

- Table Etiquette
- Learn Laundry Symbols
- How to Read a Recipe
- How to Iron Clothes
- How to Study
- How to Pump Gas

BEAUTIFULLY ORGANIZED

In each space, follow these five essential steps for organization success:

STEP ONE: ASSESS

The first step is one that requires more thought than action, but it is vital to your long-term success. Begin by asking yourself these questions: What is the purpose of this space? Am I making the best use of it? Do my family and I have any needs that may be served by using this area differently? How might I adapt this space so that it functions well?

Here's an example: I once worked with clients who had a lovely formal dining room. However, the family only used the room once or twice a year for holiday meals. Meanwhile, the husband worked from home on a tiny desk in the corner of the master bedroom. His files and notes—not to mention the hum of the computer monitor—intruded into what should be a peaceful room. Ultimately, my clients realized their home would be more functional (and happier!) if they adapted their dining room so it could also be utilized as a home office.

STEP TWO: DECLUTTER

Decluttering is by far the most daunting step in the process. However, it is also the step that gives you the greatest feeling of accomplishment when you've finished. Before you can think about implementing new systems in a space, it is imperative to first get rid of unwanted, unnecessary, or duplicative items.

Before you jump into decluttering, however, it is helpful to think about what has led you to accumulate items in the first place. If you recognize the underlying causes of your clutter, you will feel empowered as you begin to declutter and less likely to fall into the same pattern in the future.

◁ CAUSES OF CLUTTER ▷

The reasons we accumulate clutter may be complex and varied, but it often boils down to this: we create an attachment to certain items and this makes it difficult to release the items from our homes. These are a few reasons people are reluctant to get rid of things:

Sentimental Syndrome

Emotional attachment is the most common reason I encounter when people feel compelled to keep unwanted or unneeded things. Some people even feel a sense of obligation to things given to them by others—sometimes even when those items actually make them unhappy! If you feel as though you must keep gifts that were given to you, consider that the person who gave you that gift had the intention to make you happy. If they knew that the gift was no longer bringing you joy, I am convinced that they would want you to pass it along.

Also consider that there are people in need who may be able to use items that do not serve a purpose in your home. Knowing that your unused items will make a positive impact in someone else's life may make it easier to release yourself from your possessions.

"I May Need It Later" Syndrome

I asked a friend why she had eight different wooden spoons in her kitchen. Her response was, "I may need them one day." I cannot imagine a situation in which she would need eight wooden spoons! Many times, I find that people keep items with the intent to use them one day, but rarely actually do so.

I recommend that you give yourself strict limitations. Incorporate an "only one backup" rule. In other words, you allow yourself just one back-up item for anything in your home. This way, you accommodate the desire to be prepared without overdoing it.

Shopping Habit

You can order almost anything and have it delivered to your front porch in twenty-four hours—or less! The ease of one-click shopping causes many consumers to overindulge. On top of that, we are constantly bombarded with billboards, internet ads, and television commercials that insist we need more. It can be difficult to resist this temptation, even when impulsive purchases rarely result in long-term happiness.

Learned Behavior

I chuckle to myself sometimes when I recognize that I have truly turned into my mother. It turns out that what I observed as a child now influences me as an adult. My mother kept a beautiful home and she loved to entertain. Her home featured elegant white furniture and décor, and she had a natural, graceful way of making her guests feel special. I strive to incorporate her style and manner into my home and life. However, what if I had grown up observing the opposite? What if I lived in a chaotic, disorganized home? If so, I may have a much different perspective as an adult. Your own home and habits may be influenced by what you learned. The good news is that if your current situation is less-than-ideal, this book will help you to approach your home with a fresh perspective!

Feeling Overwhelmed

As a professional organizer, the question I hear most often from family, friends, and clients is, "How do I begin to get my home in order?" It can be incredibly frustrating to come home each day to a messy house that lacks a sense of peace and order. Often, when we are exhausted and faced with an overwhelming task (such as tidying a messy home), we just shut down. It is easier to ignore the problem—even if it makes us unhappy—if we don't know how to solve it. That is why the steps and processes I outline in this book are so important: they give you concrete, practical ways to organize your home—and to keep it organized!

Which of these "causes of clutter" do you identify with? Remember, understanding the underlying cause of your clutter is half the battle! Decluttering your space does not have to be traumatic. Rather, once you get over the attachment hurdle (and you will!), decluttering will leave you feeling lighter and happier as you release yourself from unneeded things.

◁ HOW TO DECLUTTER ▷

Decluttering can *feel* like a slog, but it doesn't have to! I have a few tips and tricks to make the decluttering process efficient and—dare I say it—fun!

A Decluttering Station

My best advice is to set up a decluttering station. This is a must! Find three large containers; ideally, these will be found around your home. Laundry baskets or even large trash bags are perfect. Label each bin or bag with the words "purge," "keep," and "donate." Place the bins or bags in the center of the room you plan to work in.

The decluttering station will keep you focused and help you to work toward a target number of items to remove from the space. I will say it again for emphasis: it is crucial that you do not start the decluttering process without setting up this system. To proceed without a station in place creates the risk of making an even bigger mess as you pull items from cabinets and drawers. Falling into this trap may reduce your motivation and stall your progress.

DECLUTTERING GUIDE

START HERE

DO YOU NEED IT? — NO → DO YOU LOVE IT? — NO →

YES

YES

DOES IT HAVE VALUE?

ARE YOU EMOTIONALLY ATTACHED?

NO

YES   NO   YES

IS IT STILL USEFUL?

KEEP ← YES — DOES IT FIT THE SPACE?

NO   YES

NO

DO YOU KNOW SOME-ONE WHO COULD USE IT?

IS IT A FAMILY HEIRLOOM? — NO

YES   NO

YES

NO

SELL

CAN YOU TRANSFER TO A FAMILY MEMBER

PURGE

DONATE

YES

TAKE TO THEM ←

Make it Fun

While cleaning out a closet on a Saturday afternoon isn't exactly the dictionary definition of "fun," decluttering doesn't have to be an exercise in misery. Listen to a podcast or daydream about what your space will look like when it's spruced up.

Another great option is to invite a friend to help you. A good friend can offer advice and perspective and can even serve as a "reality check" when you need it. ("Have you ever worn those ridiculously high heels?!")

Set a Time Limit

Don't give yourself too much time to think about whether you need to keep an item. The purging process needs to be quick and to the point. Allow yourself three seconds per item. The more time that you give yourself to think about an item, the more likely you are to hold on to it.

Play Music

When I listen to certain music, I feel happy and pumped. It makes me want to move! Make a playlist with upbeat, energetic music to make the purging process flow faster. You can also use music as your timer by setting a goal to have your purging station filled by the time a song is finished.

Remove Purged Items Immediately

I am a stickler about this rule, too. When you schedule time to declutter a room, be sure to include enough time to remove the purged items from your home. All of the items in the donation bin should be taken to the donation center. (At a minimum, the items should be moved to the trunk of your car!) If you have borrowed items to return to family or friends or purchased items that need to be returned to the store, move these items directly to your vehicle and return them the next time you leave the house. If you plan to sell items in a yard sale, tag the items with a price and place them in an area designated for yard sale staging.

In short, the garage, basement, or attic should never be used to store items purged during decluttering. Simply relocating items from one space to another is counterproductive and stunts your progress toward making your home beautifully organized!

STEP THREE: *CLEAN*

Once the purging party is over, there are sure to be a few hidden dust bunnies that come out of hiding. If you do not already have a mini cleaning caddy, this is the perfect time to create one. A mini cleaning caddy will make it easy for you to clean on the go. I recommend that your caddy includes only items essential to accomplish the tasks at hand.

◁ *CREATE A MINI CLEANING CADDY* ▷

The perfect cleaning caddy can be beautiful. Yes, I said beautiful! Gone are the days of the ugly blue bucket with a yellow sponge. Given the choice, who would want to clean with cleaning supplies that scream, "You are about to do some *work!*"? Instead, when you put together your caddy, consider the function *and* the overall look of the caddy. I believe that if an item is going to take up space in your home, it should be beautiful. Embracing this concept will help you to create a consistent, fresh, and beautiful theme throughout every nook and cranny of your home. If you see a beautiful caddy when you open your cabinet, you are one step closer to a more enjoyable home cleaning session.

Cleaning Gloves

Cleaning can take a toll on your hands; cleaning gloves will keep those hands beautiful. Gloves also give you the perfect opportunity to pamper yourself with a beauty treatment as you clean. Rub a luxurious lotion on your hands and put on a pair of white gloves. Then, wear your cleaning gloves over the white gloves. When you are finished cleaning, your hands will be radiant and soft rather than tired and worn.

Microfiber Cloths

Microfiber cloths are the MVP of my cleaning caddy; they are a must-have item. The fibers in these cloths naturally pick up dust from the surfaces they come in contact with, so a lot of the work is done for you. Microfiber cloths can be used wet or dry; either method will attract dust.

TIP

Select microfiber cloths in a color you love. When I see anything teal, I feel inspired. This enhances my desire to clean, even if slightly!

Cleaning Toothbrushes

For years, detail cleaning brushes have been my favorite cleaning tools. The toothbrushes aren't fancy, merely inexpensive soft-bristle toothbrushes. They are great for cleaning around faucets, light switches, and all those hard-to-reach spots. I have a toothbrush labeled "electronic" for cleaning remote controls and other devices, a dedicated "bathroom" toothbrush used to remove scum from behind the faucet and along grout lines, a "decor" brush for items like ornate vases, and finally, a soft-bristle brush for cleaning silver.

Cleaning Products

There are two primary products you need in your mini cleaning caddy: a glass cleaner and an all-purpose cleaner. These are a perfect team to get you through the majority of your cleaning.

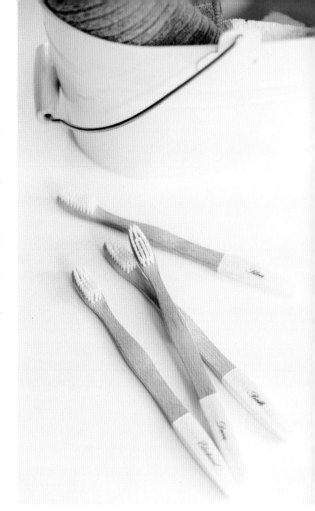

TIP

You can make inexpensive glass cleaner and all-purpose cleaner at home using natural ingredients. Try these recipes:

GLASS CLEANER:
1 cup of white vinegar + 1 cup of rubbing alcohol +
one cup of water

ALL-PURPOSE CLEANER:
1 cup of white vinegar + 1 cup of water +
20-30 drops of your favorite essential oil

Eraser Pad

I have nicknamed the eraser pad "the miracle pad." I have never seen a pad able to remove marks and dirt with such ease. It is a must-have item for your cleaning caddy.

Once you have thoroughly decluttered a space, take the time to clean it well. Wipe down shelves, baseboards, and any other surfaces that could use a little sparkle. Clean the windows and vacuum the floors. This will propel you into step four with a feeling of accomplishment!

STEP FOUR: ORGANIZE

Remember when you assessed your space back in step one? Now is the time to recall any new ways you would like to approach your space. Your ultimate goal is to have a sensible place for everything that belongs in this area. Here are some things to consider as you put things away:

▶ Are you making the best use of the space available to you? Are you maximizing the space you have?

▷ Have you placed frequently-used items someplace accessible? These items should be easy to locate—and easy to put away when you're finished with them!

▷ If an item isn't often used, can you store the item in an intuitive location?

There are a variety of simple, effective tricks and "systems" to organize your belongings. These are some of the approaches I use successfully with client after client, as well as in my own home:

◁ *LABELING* ▷

I purchased my first label maker over twenty years ago for just ten dollars. I still have it, and it has been one of the most useful tools I have ever purchased for my home! Labels can be utilized to help maintain your home's organization, subtle prompts to encourage family members to return items to their appropriate places. However, I caution you not to over-label! You do not want your home to look like an instruction manual. There are creative ways to discreetly label your spaces *and* maintain your home's beauty:

Shelf Top Labeling
Place your labels on the top surface of the cabinet shelving instead of on the outer edge of the cabinet. The labels are then hidden from direct view.

Built-in Labeling
Purchase organizers that incorporate a built-in label option. This built-in feature will make labeling an item feel more natural.

Decorative Labeled Organizers
There are times when using a label-maker is not the most elegant option! There are

many beautifully designed, pre-labeled storage options on the market. These items often feature decorative writing and accents to identify what goes in the container. My dog's pet food container is a good example: I wanted to avoid an un-attractive plastic pet food bin and I didn't want to place a label on a container. As always, I desired both function and beauty. I opted for a lovely custom canister with my dog's name on it, along with a comple-mentary "dog treats" canister.

◁ OTHER ORGANIZATIONAL METHODS ▷

Color Coding Method

Color coding can be an excellent, aesthetically appealing way to categorize things in your home to make them easy to identify. For example, I store all of my Christmas items in red bins. Color coding also works well when organizing items for multiple children. Each child can be assigned a color for his or her storage containers. Even children who cannot yet read will be able to recognize their assigned colors.

Visual Method

One of the easiest ways to make items visible and accessible without "labeling" is to use transparent organizers that allow you to see items in their containers. This method is particularly useful when organizing spaces that frequently change, such as your refrigerator.

STEP FIVE: *BEAUTIFY*

This step is purely enjoyable. You have reimagined your space and done the hard work to declutter, purge items, clean, and implement new systems to keep your be-longings in their places. Now you can focus on the finishing touches that make your home beautiful and unique to you and your family. Of course, what appeals to one person won't necessarily appeal to another, so beautifying your space is a highly per-sonal undertaking. When I work with clients, I encourage them to engage all of their senses as they select beautiful elements to soften and warm their homes.

◁ *SIGHT* ▷

Furniture, rugs, artwork, and other home décor items are often costly. It's wise to devote time to defining your own personal style before you invest in expensive pieces for your home.

TIP

Browse home décor magazines or books (or Pinterest!) for visual inspiration and motivation.

What inspires you? What details speak to you? It may be the color palette used in the space; it may be the minimalist approach or the cheerful bohemian look. Hone your style and then bring it to your home décor. Remember: you don't have to copy a room in a catalog page. Think about what truly brings you joy. Do you have a fabulous piece of artwork or a treasured book collection? Focus on what is important to you to kick start your creativity as you beautify your space.

◁ *SOUND* ▷

Sound is often an overlooked element in homes. We tend to notice sound when something is particularly annoying—a refrigerator that hums too loudly or a clock that ticks obnoxiously. While it's important to try to eliminate unpleasant, distracting noises, have you considered that sound can also enhance your enjoyment of your home?

Music

While high-end homes may feature built-in speaker systems throughout the house, there is a quick and easy way to achieve a similar effect: install speaker light bulbs into your lamp to easily enjoy music throughout your home. Make sure the bulbs are balanced throughout your space so that sound travels evenly.

Candles

I'm sure you are wondering what candles have to do with sound! I love to use candles to create a cozy atmosphere, and it's not just about the flickering lights. Candles with a wood wick create a sound similar to a crackling fireplace!

Sound Machines

Sound machines offer subtle background noise that can bring a feeling of calm to a space. You may live in the desert, but the sound of waves can make you feel as if your home is on oceanfront property!

◁ *TASTE* ▷

I like to keep simple mints and candies in decorative jars—tiny indulgences for me, as well as for my guests!

Years ago, a friend told me that she places a bowl of nuts out when she has visitors. This gives her a way to subtly detect if her guests are hungry. If the bowl is quickly emptied, she knows to offer something more substantial to satisfy appetites!

◁ *SCENT* ▷

Scent plays a big role in how we experience our homes, as well as in how other people perceive our homes. If a home smells, it speaks volumes about the cleanliness of that house. However, the chemical smell of certain cleaning products can be just as unpleasant! There are so many natural ways to clean your home that don't involve overpowering, often toxic smells.

Eliminate Odors

▶ TRASH Take out your trash each day to keep foul odors at bay. When I put a new trash bag into the can, I like to put a few shakes of baking soda into the bottom of the bag to help control odor. (There are also trash bags on the market that incorporate baking soda.) You should also clean your garbage can from time to time, even if you use trash bag liners.

▶ DIRTY LAUNDRY Piles of dirty laundry carry a stale, unpleasant odor. Use a laundry schedule so that dirty clothes don't pile up for longer than necessary. (*I share my favorite tips for managing laundry in Chapter Ten.*)

▶ GARBAGE DISPOSAL The garbage disposal is a work horse—and it smells like it! It's important to deodorize and sanitize the garbage disposal weekly. We love our lemonade here in the south; I am always using leftover lemon rinds to clean my disposal; the fresh lemon scent is an added bonus! I also grind ice in the disposal to help keep the blades sharp.

While managing and minimizing unpleasant odors is the first, most important thing to address, there are also a variety of ways to bring pleasant scents into your home:

Let Your Home Breathe

Whenever possible, open your windows and doors to allow fresh air to circulate throughout your home. I also recommend investing in an air purifier to use during colder months. Just as we need fresh air for healthy bodies, we need fresh air for healthy homes.

Fresh Flowers and Plants

Fresh flowers and plants add natural beauty to the home. Many houseplants actually purify the air in your house! Plants are also budget-friendly—or at least they are if you have a green thumb. (I don't!)

It can be expensive to keep fresh flowers in your home all the time. However, if your outdoor space allows, consider planting perennial flowers that bloom at different times. This way, you will always have access to fresh flowers!

Embrace a Signature Scent

To avoid assaulting your sense of smell, consider buying products with a consistent scent. For example, I use Caldrea® products, including dishwasher detergent, countertop spray, and hand soap. The subtle, natural scent creates a consistent and pleasant aroma throughout my house.

◁ TOUCH ▷

As you incorporate elements to create warmth and beauty in your home, consider how to creatively engage the sense of touch.

Textiles

Throw pillows come in endless varieties; mix and match sizes and textures for visual interest and comfort. A plush area rug can feel wonderful under the feet. A soft throw blanket over the arm of a sofa is cozy and inviting.

Other "Touchables"

I like to keep touchable items around my home to engage family and friends when they visit. For example, I keep a marble tic-tac-toe game on my patio table. It's a simple yet beautiful object and it is a highlight of the space when we entertain.

CREATE AN EXPERIENCE

I believe that our homes provide so many opportunities to create wonderful, life-long memories. Putting forth the effort to beautifully organize is absolutely worthwhile. However, I also believe that you have the opportunity to go a step further to create truly memorable experiences for yourself and the people you cherish. To this end, many of the chapters in this book include tips to "Create an Experience" in a given space. These "Wow!" moments are ways to add something to excite your family or guests.

You have read about many of my processes, tips, and tricks to create and maintain a pleasant, functional home. Of course, each space in the home presents its own unique challenges and considerations. Let's go room-by-room to discover more about how to make your home beautifully organized!

CHAPTER TWO

ENTRYWAY

The First Impression Space

Would a professional organizer ever hire another professional organizer to help organize her home? Sound crazy? Absolutely not! I have a client who is a talented and successful home organizer. The truth is that we *all* have tough spaces in our homes that we cannot figure out. It is smart to get fresh eyes and a new perspective on these places. You can ask a friend or a family member—or even a professional organizer!

This particular client has a beautiful home, but she struggled with her entryway. This area was a catch-all for her entire family. The kids would come home from school, kick their shoes off in front of the door, and toss their coats on the floor. This chaotic scene greeted her when she arrived home from work each evening. After several failed attempts to implement systems to keep the space in order, my client was frustrated.

Before we touched a thing in her entryway, we first needed to create buy-in from the family. With any communal space in your home, the secret to success is to have your entire family committed to keeping the space in order. I know—it sounds like an impossible mission. We all have different priorities. In this case, the children's preference was to get their shoes and coats off as quickly as possible to get to the kitchen for a snack. A beautiful, clutter-free entryway was not even on the kids' radar. This was the perfect opportunity to hold a Family Home Meeting as described in the last chapter.

My client embraced the FHM. She assigned one child a one-week task to remind everyone in the family to put their shoes and coats away. By giving this leadership role to her child, my client was one step closer to family buy-in for a clutter-free entryway. Will her children appreciate that shoes are no longer piled in front of the door? Perhaps not, but they will develop an understanding of family expectations and accountability for keeping the space in order. As cliché as it sounds, communication was the key to solving the entryway enigma for this particular client!

Once my client was able to work through this issue and help her family to develop new habits, she enjoyed the process of setting up a beautiful, organized dream entryway.

———————◇———————

I like to call the entryway the "First Impression Space" of my home because it is the first area our guests experience when they visit. Of course, while it's wonderful to create a great first impression for guests, it is also true that your home's entryway is the last area you see as you leave for a day in this crazy world and it is the first space that you encounter when you arrive back home. The entryway plays a considerable role in setting the tone for your entire house; thought should go into making this space function well and to making it aesthetically pleasing.

Entryways come in all shapes and sizes, but I find that requirements for how the space functions are typically similar. As such, my approach to organizing the entryway space is fairly universal—and I do insist that the space should be functional *and* beautiful!

STEP ONE: ASSESS YOUR ENTRYWAY

As I discussed in chapter one, the first step toward a beautifully organized home is to assess your space objectively. Think about your entryway. Do you maintain a shoe-free home and therefore need a dedicated place to store shoes as you enter the house? Do you need to store a dog leash, or does your family need a dumping ground for keys and mail? It is important to consider your needs so that you can put the appropriate systems in place for you and your family.

Each person has everyday essentials they rely on: keys, handbags, backpacks, umbrellas, and so forth. These items are necessary, but they can clutter up your entryway. Consider your daily needs but try to minimize the overall number of things that are stored in the entryway space.

A small entryway is challenging because of space constraints; a grand entryway can become overrun with piles of clutter. With planning, a dash of style, and a willingness to think outside the box, you can have a beautifully organized entryway, no matter the size.

STEP TWO: DECLUTTER YOUR ENTRYWAY

I have helped to organize hundreds of homes; in my experience, the same types of items clutter the entryway:

◁ *MAIL* ▷

It's easy to understand why mail piles up in the entryway: you arrive home, grab the mail from the mailbox, and hold it in your hand as you cross the threshold. You drop the mail to remove your coat and shoes, and then you're suddenly greeting your family, setting the table, or helping with a homework question. The mail remains where you left it—piled together with several days' worth of mail.

Paper clutter is a big problem in many homes and mail pile-up is often the culprit. Remember, the entryway is a communal area. You can develop good habits to control paper clutter. I advise my clients to take immediate action with their mail. Here's a rule of thumb: don't let the mail touch a table or countertop! Train yourself to quickly sort the mail as soon as you collect it. Toss junk mail in the recycling bin or run it through the shredder. Place newly arrived magazines next to your reading chair; transfer bills or other important paperwork to your home office (see chapter six). This process takes only a minute or two each day!

◁ SHOPPING BAGS ▷

Shopping bags are often stored in the entryway. Reusable bags prevent an accumulation of paper bags and they're best for the environment. Keep only the number of bags needed for a single shopping trip.

◁ UMBRELLAS ▷

If I had a nickel for every broken umbrella I have removed from a client's home! As you declutter, keep only enough functional umbrellas for the members of your household, and perhaps an extra umbrella or two for houseguests to borrow.

◁ SHOES ▷

Are you like my client from the beginning of this chapter, frustrated when you trip over a pile of shoes as you walk in the door? Try setting a limit for the number of pairs of shoes each family member can keep in the entryway. (Hint: it should be no more than two pairs per family member!)

STEP THREE: CLEAN YOUR ENTRYWAY

Cleaning is cleaning—there isn't always a lot of room for creativity! There are, however, a few products and tools that might be particularly helpful for the entryway:

◁ SHOE DEODORIZER ▷

Stinky shoes are unpleasant—not a smell you want to encounter when you walk in the door. Consider treating shoes with shoe deodorizer or baking soda to eliminate unpleasant odors. Cedar sachets are another great option to keep your shoe cabinet or closet smelling fresh.

◁ *PAW WIPES* ▷

If you have a pet that goes outside, keep wipes near the door to clean pet paws after a walk.

◁ *ROBOTIC VACUUM* ▷

As a high-traffic area, dirt accumulates quickly in the entryway. A robotic vacuum will relieve you of the task of sweeping or vacuuming the floors; push a button and your work is done! There are several affordable robotic vacuum models on the market.

◁ *SHOES IN THE HOUSE* ▷

While it's all but impossible to avoid tracking dirt into the entryway, it is possible to minimize the spread of dust into the rest of the home by maintaining a shoe-free home. However, this is one of the most controversial home-related topics I encounter as a professional organizer. Some people feel it is rude to ask guests to remove their shoes before coming into their home, while others believe that it is disrespectful to enter someone's home with shoes on. Your home is *your* personal haven, which ultimately means that you get to decide for you and your family.

If you choose to make your home shoe-free, it can feel awkward to ask your guests to remove their shoes. However, I have found that once guests understand that you do not wear shoes in the house, they are respectful of your space. There are some simple ways to convey to your guests that your home is shoe-free and to make everyone feel at home and comfortable:

Be a Director

When a guest arrives at my home for the first time, I greet them and kindly direct them where to put their shoes. I find that most guests immediately take the hint and remove their shoes.

Give a Sign

You can purchase or make a "No Shoes" sign and place it on the exterior of your residence or just inside the door. There is no guarantee that your guests will notice the sign; you may need to be more direct.

STEP FOUR: ORGANIZE YOUR ENTRYWAY

The entryway is a high-traffic area. I recommend a minimalist approach to your entryway to enhance both the function and the aesthetics of the space, creating a feeling of welcome. Here are some things to consider:

◁ CLOSET ▷

Not every home has an entryway closet. If you have one, you have struck gold! The entryway closet is a great opportunity to use color coding. Assign a different color to each family member and provide hangers and bins in each color. Color coding makes it simple to beautifully organize items in a shared space like an entryway closet.

◁ SHOES ▷

If you are going to successfully eliminate the dreaded shoe pile, it's critical to designate a place to store shoes. In fact, you can go so far as to establish a "no shoes in front of the door" rule (use your family home meeting to bring this up!). The entryway closet is an ideal place to store shoes. If you do not have a closet, you can store shoes in a cabinet or bins assigned to each family member.

◁ KEYS ▷

Make a promise to yourself that you will never again scramble to find your keys in the morning! Organizing keys in your entryway is simple. You can discreetly place your keys behind a framed tabletop picture on your entryway table. Or, use a decorative lidded box or attractive bowl or basket as a catch-all for keys. You might prefer to install a key hook on the inside of your entryway closet door. I prefer to place my keys directly in my handbag; this makes sense for me as I never go anywhere without both of these items!

◁ EVERYDAY ITEMS ▷

I love to use decorative magazine holders to store umbrellas, leashes, and other random items! These narrow holders are great space savers and can be placed atop or inside a cabinet, or inside an entryway closet.

◁ CABINET OR TABLE ▷

If space permits, a cabinet or table offers excellent storage for the entryway. Think about the items you need to store and the available space; these considerations will help you to identify the ideal size and specifications for furniture pieces.

In the hustle and bustle of the morning, it's easy to forget a needed item as you rush out the door. If you're like me and your brain wakes up at 10am (even if your body wakes up at 7am!), it can be helpful to place a "forget-me-not" basket in the entryway. This is an area to place anything you need to remember as you leave the house, a centralized checkpoint that offers an easy way to avoid a frantic search for overdue library books or field trip permission slips.

◁ BENCH ▷

An entryway storage bench offers dual function: a place to sit to put on or remove your shoes and a way to conceal shoes, bags, or other items. Benches with individual compartments are ideal for families; each family member can have their own section or bin.

STEP FIVE: *BEAUTIFY* YOUR ENTRYWAY

There are many opportunities to bring warmth and soul to your entryway while simultaneously meeting everyone's needs. Home décor items can be both functional and beautiful; they give you a way to infuse your unique personality into the entryway and to make walking through the front door a pleasurable experience.

◁ LIGHTING ▷

Good entryway lighting is essential. Whether a chandelier or a table lamp, you should have an attractive light source to illuminate the space and create a welcoming ambiance.

◁ PLANT LIFE ▷

Plants (even artificial ones!) give a sense of growth and life to a space; they are ideal decor for an entryway. Plants add beauty, but they can also be a clever way to hide extra keys, the wifi password, or alarm codes. A humble houseplant can provide a discreet way to keep valuable items and information right at your fingertips.

◁ *MIRROR* ▷

Mirrors come in all shapes and sizes, and many are quite beautiful. A mirror will bounce light around a space, making it look larger than it is. A mirror in the entryway is also useful to check your appearance as you dash out the door.

◁ *DECORATIVE ACCESSORIES* ▷

Smart, decorative accessories like lidded boxes or woven baskets offer both function and beauty, a way to store your items and make your entryway sparkle with personality.

◁ *RUGS* ▷

Rugs are an excellent addition to warm up the entryway space (and to catch dirt before it is tracked into your house). Select a rug that fits the size of your entryway; an out-of-scale rug could make the space feel awkward.

I challenge you to think beyond simply having a place to hang your coat and store your shoes. Create a beautifully organized entryway as a highlight of your home!

CREATE AN EXPERIENCE

◇

I believe that in almost every space in your home, there is an opportunity to create a warm and welcoming experience for the family and friends you welcome as guests. This is certainly true for the entryway! After all, this is where you first greet your guests. As you organize your entryway, consider what will make your guests feel welcomed and relaxed when they arrive at your home. Your home should be filled with love, warmth, and positivity, and this starts at the front door.

◁ *GUEST SOCKS OR SLIPPERS* ▷

Provide fresh, clean socks or slippers for guests to create a welcoming and relaxing vibe in your space. These do not need to be expensive; you can find reasonably priced options at local discount stores. Place the socks or slippers in a basket in your entryway when you are expecting guests; you can even wrap the socks or slippers with an attractive ribbon labeled with the size.

◁ COMFORT STATION ▷

My husband and I frequently host out-of-town guests. We live in beautiful Charleston, South Carolina, and our guests often like to explore the city. I have a drawer in my entryway cabinet that is dedicated to items to make my guests feel comfortable during their stay. I keep extra throw blankets, a few spare umbrellas, and to-go beverage tumblers. These items make our guests feel cared for and welcomed.

◁ GIFTS ▷

I also keep a selection of small gifts in a drawer in my entryway cabinet. I can access these items any time I want to make a guest feel special. It is a warm feeling to be able to give your guest a little parting gift as they leave your home. Keep a supply of decadent dark chocolate bars, tiny bottles of champagne, or any other treat that strikes your fancy! (These small but thoughtful gifts are also great if you have a guest and you realize that they recently celebrated a birthday or anniversary. Having a mini built-in gift shop comes in handy!)

The key to success is to incorporate entryway essentials in an eye-pleasing way into whatever space welcomes you, your family, and friends into your home. Have fun and be creative as you establish workable systems, even with space constraints!

HOW TO CREATE A
SMALL-SPACE ENTRYWAY

We would all love to have a grand entryway that can easily and gracefully accommodate all of the items we would like to store in the space. However, this is not the reality for many of us! In some homes, you walk right into a living area as you open the door. This was true in several houses we have lived in over the years. When you live in a small space, the key to successfully organizing your entryway area is to be creative in your thought process. You need to think outside of the box. I want to share some options for adapting some of the systems I discussed earlier in this chapter in small spaces.

▶ SHOE STORAGE If you don't have a place for your family and guest to store their shoes, I challenge you to examine your space more closely and get creative. When we lived in New Jersey, calling our home a shoe box was an apt metaphor. The sofa was right beside the front door. This meant that we used the space under the couch as a "shoe cabinet." It was a vacant space and kept the shoes out of the walkway.

▶ WALL SHELVES Utilizing vertical space is my go-to solution in small spaces. Walls can be your hero when you live in a small house! Consider installing beautiful wall shelves just inside your front door. Add attractive bins or baskets that can hold entryway essentials; you can even store shoes on the lower shelves.

▶ COATS If you lack an entryway closet, place a coat rack or install decorative wall hooks near the front door.

CHAPTER THREE

KITCHEN
The Meeting Space

I always emphasize to my clients that their home needs to fit their lifestyle. As I work in many different homes, I am struck by how people hold onto items they do not use or have spaces configured in a way that does not serve their needs. For example, if nobody in your house drinks coffee, you probably don't need a coffee maker on the countertop taking up valuable space.

One of my clients—a mother to two little girls who was expecting another child and whose husband was deployed by the military—was so frustrated by her kitchen pantry. Her home was organized and clean, but when I opened her pantry door, I found a disaster zone. Although the shelves were messy, at first glance, the items appeared to belong. Dry goods, canned foods, and other food items overflowed from the shelves.

The first step was to talk with my client to gain an understanding of her family's day-to-day life. This young mother handled all of her family's logistics: keeping track of appointments, paying bills, planning and cooking meals, and so forth. I also learned that while she cooked dinner in the evenings, she would keep the children occupied with craft projects at the kitchen table.

As we looked around her kitchen space, I noted that she had massive amounts of cabinet space—plenty of space in which to conveniently store food items. I realized that we could work together to make my client's kitchen and pantry space more functional. We relocated food items from the pantry to a large expanse of kitchen cupboards. This made the food much more accessible, saving my client trips back and forth from the kitchen to the pantry as she prepared meals. (This is no small thing for a busy mom!) It also freed the pantry space to be used differently. We created a "command station" in the pantry, a beautiful mini-office to house the essentials to manage her home. We included a craft area to store bins filled with craft supplies for the kids. We designated a space for my client's cookbooks, easy to access as she planned meals. We also set up a station for organizing bills and a large calendar to track appointments and other events. Of course, everything was beautifully coordinated in her favorite color. For months after the project was complete, my client would tell me how this small space in her home gave her so much happiness.

———————◇———————

The kitchen is one of the most important spaces in my home. It's not that I am a master chef (that is definitely not the case!), but rather it's because our kitchen is truly the hub of the home. It is where we nourish our love for each other—a space that feeds

our souls *and* our bellies. To maximize our enjoyment of this space, it's essential that it is well-organized and functional. However, in every room in the house, I believe there is an opportunity to create a space that is beautifully organized, and the kitchen is no exception.

STEP ONE: ASSESS YOUR KITCHEN

At the most basic level, a kitchen space needs to be well-planned simply because one needs to be able to maneuver efficiently. Since kitchens tend to have many cabinets, they can become easily cluttered and filled with things that you do not need. I have moved many times over the years; with each move, setting up my kitchen has always been one of my first priorities. With all this practice, I have created a structured process to implement organization in this important space.

It can be tricky to envision how and where to place all the items in your kitchen sensibly. As you begin to plan your kitchen's organization, think about how you and your family use the space. Your organization plan should enable you to function in the way that suits your lifestyle. Whether your kitchen is big or small, know that kitchens of all sizes benefit from a well-thought organization plan. Here are some things to consider:

▶ What is the primary purpose of your kitchen? The answer may differ from home to home. If you love to cook or bake, your kitchen setup will look different from a home where the family often dines out.

▶ What are your entertaining needs? If you frequently entertain guests in your kitchen, you should set up the space to be guest-friendly. For example, you might consider stocking a beverage bar so that guests can help themselves at their leisure. Also, give thought to the number of dishes you store in your cabinets. Frequent guests = a need for more dishes!

STEP TWO: *DECLUTTER* YOUR KITCHEN

With its cabinets and drawers, nooks and crannies, the kitchen tends to be a black hole. Items find their way to the kitchen, never to be seen again! When you initially declutter your kitchen, you may be amazed by what you find stored in the back of your cabinets. However, decluttering the kitchen needs to be an ongoing process—it is rarely a "one and done" undertaking. In other words, you should continually ask yourself if the items in your kitchen still serve a purpose. These items accumulate in many kitchens:

◁ *RANDOM LIDS* ▷

How often do you come across a lid that has no matching container? Remove any lids that lack a partner.

◁ *EXTRA COOKING TOOLS* ▷

Here's a quick quiz: how many can openers do you own? As I mentioned in chapter one, I am always amazed by the number of cooking tools in most home kitchens—more

than enough to outfit a busy restaurant kitchen! Extra cooking utensils act as barriers that keep you from accessing the items you need. Try to limit yourself to only the tools that you truly use in your kitchen.

◁ RANDOM GADGETS ▷

I love a kitchen gadget. They are my weakness—I admit it. Kitchen gadgets have a way of drawing us in because they promise a way to make life easier. In reality, in the kitchen, the endgame is to get meals prepared as quickly and efficiently as possible. It isn't usually convenient to search for a fancy gadget that is used for a single purpose when a basic tool will suffice. While gadgets are fun, they are space snatchers and should be removed from the kitchen if they are not frequently used.

◁ EXPIRED FOOD ▷

It's important to understand the shelf life for foods that you commonly store to make sure that the food is safe and edible. As you declutter your kitchen, check the dates on cans and spices and discard any expired items. For food that doesn't have an expiration date on the label, reference the chart on page 60 to help you decide if something needs to be thrown away. If you're not sure if an item has reached the end of its shelf life, it is best to err on the side of caution!

PANTRY SHELF LIFE

PRODUCT	SHELF LIFE	PRODUCT	SHELF LIFE
Baking Powder	12 months	Marshmallows	3 months
Baking Soda	24 months	Mayonnaise	4 months – unopened 2 months – opened, in fridge
Beans & Peas – dried	18 months	Milk – evaporated	12 months – unopened
Biscuit Mix	12-18 months	Milk – powdered, non-fat	12-24 months
Bread Crumbs	2-4 months	Milk – sweetened condensed	12 months
Cookie/Cake Mix	12 months	Mustard	24 months – unopened 12 months – opened, in fridge
Canned Fruit	12 months	Nuts – unshelled	8 months
Canned Meat	12 months	Oils – Canola, Vegetable, Corn	1-2 years – unopened 6-8 months – after opening
Canned Vegetables	12 months	Oils – Olive	24 months
Cereals – dried	2-3 months	Onions	4-6 weeks
Cereals – hot	12 months	Pancake Mix	6 months
Chocolate – unsweetened	18 months	Pasta – dried	24 months
Chocolate Chips – semi-sweet	12 months	Peanut Butter	6-9 months
Cocoa Powder	24 months	Pickles, Olives, Relish	1 year – unopened 3 months – opened, in fridge
Coconut – shredded	12 months	Popcorn – microwave	6-8 months
Coffee – ground	3-5 months	Popcorn – kernels	12-24 months
Coffee – instant	24 months	Potatoes – instant	12 months
Coffee – whole bean	6 months	Potatoes – white or sweet	3-5 weeks
Cookies – packaged	2-4 months	Salad Dressing	10 months – unopened 3 months – opened, in fridge
Corn Meal	12 months	Salt	Indefinitely
Corn Starch	18 months	Sauces & Condiments	12 months - unopened
Crackers	6 months	Shortening	8 months – unopened 6 months – after opening
Croutons	6 months	Soft Drinks	6 months
Flour – cake	6 months	Spices – dried, ground	12-24 months
Flour – white	10-15 months	Spices – dried, whole	24-36 months
Flour – whole wheat	6-8 months	Sports Drinks – bottled	9 months
Frosting – canned	8 months – unopened	Sugar – brown	4 months
Fruit – dried	6-8 months	Sugar – granulated	24 months
Gelatin	12-18 months	Sugar – powdered	18 months
Grits – instant	8 months	Tea – bags and loose	6-12 months
Grits – regular	10 months	Tea – instant	12 months
Honey & Syrup	12 months	Vinegar – Balsamic, Cider, Red, White, Rice	Indefinitely
Hot Chocolate Mix	6-12 months	Yeast – active dry	Follow package date
Jelly & Preserves	12 months – unopened 8 months – opened, in fridge		
Ketchup & BBQ Sauce	12 months – unopened 5 months – opened in fridge		

◁ *DAMAGED DISHES* ▷

Chipped dishes and glassware can be dangerous and should be immediately purged from your kitchen.

◁ *EXTRA CLEANING PRODUCTS* ▷

What does it look like under your kitchen sink right now? Is it a cleaning product graveyard? If so, you are not alone. The under-sink area can feel unmanageable if it is crammed with half-empty bottles of countertop spray. Pare back your cleaning supplies to only the essentials (reference "Mini Cleaning Caddy" on page 30 in chapter one) to save space in the kitchen and eliminate chaos in cleaning!

STEP THREE: *CLEAN YOUR KITCHEN*

Many people are overwhelmed by the thought of decluttering, cleaning, and organizing their kitchens. They may organize a drawer or two and then lose steam. That's understandable! With the many spaces and hundreds of items found in the kitchen,

it can take time and thought to really get your kitchen in order. Rome wasn't built in a day, and you may not be able to organize your kitchen in one day, either. It's fine if you need to take it one area at a time. Also know that because the kitchen is a room that is used multiple times per day—usually by multiple people—cleaning the kitchen must also be an ongoing process.

◁ DEEP CLEANING ▷

As you approach each space in your kitchen—whether the pantry, the refrigerator, under the sink, or cabinets and drawers—it's best to remove all items from the space, purge any items you don't use, and thoroughly clean the space before you put away the items you intend to keep. Sanitize cabinet shelves and the interior of drawers; deodorize the refrigerator with baking soda. You will feel a sense of accomplishment as your kitchen begins to gleam!

◁ DAILY CLEANING ▷

It is also important to establish daily cleaning routines and expectations for everyone who lives in your home. Again, because the kitchen is a communal area, all family members should share responsibility for keeping the space clean. This doesn't need to be complicated; a simple daily cleaning routine that suits how your family works is best.

No Dishes in the Sink Rule

This is my favorite rule! Success begins with loading the dishwasher each evening and emptying it first thing in the morning. This way, your dishwasher is empty, and family members can quickly rinse any dishes they dirty throughout the day and stack them in the dishwasher. It's a great feeling to know that you won't be greeted by a sink full of dirty dishes when you walk into the kitchen. (Hint: a Family Home Meeting topic might be "How to Load the Dishwasher." See page 23 for more about Family Home Meetings.)

Wipe Down Countertops

Just as it's a great feeling to have a sink empty of dishes, it's likewise a great feeling to have tidy countertops. Make a habit of quickly wiping up crumbs and messes from the kitchen countertops after you prepare food. Try to give the countertops a last wipe down before you go to bed at night; it's lovely to walk into a clean kitchen in the morning (and awful to begin your day by walking into a messy kitchen!).

TIP

Here's a trick to keep your kitchen sink area looking pristine: purchase a two-ring bathroom towel holder. Hang a fresh kitchen towel on the front ring; place the towel you are currently using on the back ring. Only the beautiful, clean dish towel will be visible!

STEP FOUR: ORGANIZE YOUR KITCHEN

Again, unless your kitchen is very small, you may need to clean and organize your space bit-by-bit. I recommend that you start your overall kitchen organization with the refrigerator for the simple reason that items that require refrigeration must go in that space; you aren't challenged to move items to an entirely different area. Begin with the refrigerator and then move onto other spaces in your kitchen.

◁ *REFRIGERATOR ORGANIZATION* ▷

Items stored in the refrigerator can vary from week to week, so it's important to organize your fridge in a versatile manner. Of course, staples such as eggs and milk will

have their own designated space in the fridge. However, the open shelving in refrigerators can quickly become a disaster zone if you do not have an organization system for rotating items. Consider this: an organized fridge will save you time and money. Not only will you avoid keeping the door open for five minutes while you search for the mayo, but you can also avoid buying multiple jars of the same product because you can't remember what you already have!

The "Bones" of the Refrigerator

First, create the "bones" of the refrigerator. Use organization solutions (such as clear containers) made specifically for the refrigerator. These containers come in a variety of shapes and sizes designed specifically for the refrigerator. Arrange containers to fill the majority of the space in your fridge, creating the structure to keep everything in order. The containers themselves are versatile; you may fill a container with sandwich meat one week; the next week the same container may store carrots. I do recommend that "like" items be stored together. For example, it makes sense to group sandwich ingredients (meat and cheese) in containers near one another rather than in different areas of the fridge. The key is to limit the amount of open shelf space, allowing the refrigerator to maintain its structure and items easily accessible for all members of your family. This organization strategy can be applied to your freezer, too.

Store Food with Style

I also believe in "styling" the refrigerator! It is no different than any other space in my home when it comes to incorporating beauty with function. When I open my fridge, I want it to smell fresh and look enticing.

Food packaging can take up a lot of space. I am always amazed at how much space I save in my fridge and pantry when I remove items from their store packaging. Not all things can be removed from packaging, but I do try to downsize packaging as much as possible.

MEAL TRAY PREP

Chopping onions, peeling carrots, making the marinade for the chicken: prepping dinner can take a significant amount of time. One of my favorite time-saving tricks is to prep the next day's meal as I am cooking dinner for the current evening. I recommend that you keep a "prep tray" in your refrigerator. I use simple click-and-lock food storage containers, and they are the highlight of my fridge. When dinner time rolls around, the hard part is already complete! Here is how to easily DIY a meal prep tray:

▶ **STEP ONE** Find a food-safe, refrigerator-safe tray that fits your fridge.

▶ **STEP TWO** Find smaller containers that fit on the tray. I recommend that you get a variety of sizes to accommodate the different quantities that your prep items might require.

▶ **STEP THREE** Store the meal prep tray in your fridge at all times, making it easy to access.

◁ PANTRY ORGANIZATION ▷

The pantry is a space in the kitchen that frustrates a lot of people. They find it hard to maintain; it is often filled with expired food. It can seem difficult to figure out how to organize the space so that it is functional. I recommend that you do not overthink it! Your pantry simply needs to function for *you*. Ideally, it is a place where you can quickly put away groceries and a space where the items are visible and accessible, so you can keep track of what you have and easily purge expired items. If you focus on visibility and accessibility, you will eliminate a lot of food waste.

Simple Tips to Organize Your Pantry

The first step is to remove everything from your pantry. As you remove items, sort them into different groups on your kitchen counter or table. Place items to keep in one group, items to donate in a second group, and place expired items to discard in a third group.

Next, grab a pen, paper, and a tape measure to plan the layout for your pantry. This step is essential, as you will take time to consider the space available as well as options for organizing aids. Think about different category options for food in your pantry: for example, a snack section, a section devoted to breakfast items, or a section with baking staples. Consider the number of items you typically have on hand in each category, and then plan the size and number of baskets and bins you will need to accommodate these items. It helps to measure your pantry space (including the length and width of the shelves) so that you can purchase storage containers to fit the space you have.

I also recommend labeling your baskets and bins. This is extremely helpful in keeping your pantry organized and helping your family members be able to quickly (and accurately!) identify where items belong. As with refrigerator organization, removing food items from their store packaging can save space in the pantry.

Staple food items such as rice, sugar, flour, pasta, and beans should be stored in designated containers. One beautiful and budget-friendly way to store these types of dry goods is in half-gallon mason jars. Because these jars are clear, it is easy to see how much remains in the container. You can optimally organize the mason jars by arranging the second row of jars on a two-by-four piece of wood, creating an inexpensive riser for pantry canisters.

PANTRY

BREAD

◁ KITCHEN ESSENTIALS ▷

Now that you have learned strategies to organize your food, it's time to learn how to organize the items used to prepare and present food. Cooking utensils, baking dishes, pots, and pans can quickly take over your cabinet space. Establish the number of each item you require for your kitchen to function. Many of us tend to overcompensate in our kitchens, resulting in an accumulation of items we never actually use. This can cause frustration and compromise your kitchen's aesthetic.

Cooking & Serving Utensils

As I mentioned, problems with kitchen utensils arise when you have an overabundance of tools. I want to be able to easily grab the utensil that I need. I cook often, so I store cooking utensils near my stove, beautifully displayed in a silver piece. However, I don't often bake, so I store baking utensils and tools elsewhere. For kitchen drawer storage of utensils, I love expandable bamboo organizers that allow you to customize your drawers to suit your needs; these organizers are affordable and beautiful.

Pots & Pans

It is best to keep the pots and pans you use daily nearby so they are easy to access. I love the grab-and-go method of organizing my pots and pans: this means I keep the lid and pot together so that I can grab them both in one swoop. This is not the best space saver, but it does save wear and tear on your cookware and is very convenient. If you prefer to save space, you can stack your pots and pans; however, I encourage you to invest in pan protectors if you choose this storage option.

Dishes

It's interesting to me that many people distinguish their "good" dishes from their "everyday" dishes. I do not categorize my dishes in this manner. Instead, I prefer to enjoy my beautiful dishware every day of the week. It seems silly to me to allow certain dishes to collect dust. Many evenings, my husband and I will enjoy our pizza on beautiful white (but inexpensive!) plates from Target® while drinking soda from Tiffany & Co.® wine goblets. Why not?!

I love white plates, bowls, and saucers. To me, this look is simple and classic, always elegant. These dishes make food look amazing, whether a weekday break-fast or Christmas dinner. White dinnerware is typically affordable and can be easily mixed and matched. Further, even if you are a person who loves color, the beauty in keeping white dishes is that they are so versatile. You can simply add a colorful napkin to create an entirely different look. I also love how my cabinets look when they are stacked with lovely white dishes. This truly makes for a happy kitchen!

As you organize your dishware, consider how many of each item you need to accommodate your family lifestyle. Limit the dishware you have on hand to a number that meets your daily needs. From our kitchen cabinets and the number of place settings we have on hand, one might think we are a family of twelve, when actually we are a family of two. However, I set my dishware limit to counts that accommodate our lifestyle of frequently entertaining family and friends in our home.

Kitchen Gadgets

I have already confessed that I love kitchen gadgets. I find it helpful to set a limit to prevent myself from purchasing too many enticing devices. Just as important, I make sure the gadgets I do have are easily accessible so that I will use them. The system I have in place is simple but works beautifully: I have two bins in one cabinet in which I store my gadgets. This makes it simple to find what I need. I don't allow myself to purchase more items than I can fit in these bins. I also find that storing gadgets in drawers can quickly become messy; I prefer to use bins stored in a cabinet as a neat and functional organization system.

Spice Organization

It is also challenging to keep spices organized. I admit, I struggled for years to organize my spices. Spices can be tricky because there are so many of them and it can be difficult to arrange them to be able to locate the spice you need while cooking. After years of struggle, I finally found a solution that works well: I store my spices in

a drawer next to the stove. I appreciate the convenience of keeping my spices close at hand. I use simple Ikea® jars; I label the spices and arrange them in alphabetical order, noting the expiration date on the bottom of the jar. Every time I open the drawer, it makes me happy because of the beautiful organization and the ease of use.

Of course, not every kitchen has a drawer that can accommodate spice jars. Another option is to place spice jars in a bin. Label the spices and arrange the jars in alphabetical order. The bin can be stored in a pantry or cabinet so that you can quickly and easily pull it out when needed.

The Kitchen Junk Drawer

I will come right out and say it: I am not a fan of a kitchen junk drawer. Many kitchens have one, but I think that the name alone indicates that this is not a desirable space for your beautiful home. In my kitchen, I intentionally decided to avoid falling into the junk drawer trap. However, knowing that there are definitely items that I need to access easily (if infrequently), I create a foolproof system to corral these types of items. In lieu of a junk drawer, I instead have three canisters on my kitchen counter. In the large canister, I store little bags with first aid items, matches, and so forth. In the medium canister, I store cooking thermometers; in the smallest canister, I store disposable gloves for use in the kitchen.

Recipe Organization

With the many online resources for recipes, many home cooks no longer keep cookbooks in their homes. This is not the case for my mother! She is a cookbook lover and reads them as if they are novels. It brings her joy to have her cookbooks beautifully categorized and arranged on a shelf in her kitchen. I am the total opposite. I run to my tablet when I need a new recipe and you will not find a cookbook in my home unless it is a coffee table read. I do, however, keep special recipes in the baking cabinet in my kitchen. These recipes are in a compact, personal-size planner. I laminate these recipes to keep them safe from spills and splatters. Storing favorite recipes in a small planner makes them easier to transport, and I like the idea that treasured recipes can be passed along to my children and grandchildren.

STEP FIVE: *BEAUTIFY* YOUR KITCHEN

Most of this chapter has been devoted to cleaning and organizing the kitchen. While cleaning and organizing certainly makes a space more beautiful, I think we can take it a step further! Take a moment to think about the style and colors you would like in your kitchen. I like to stick with three colors: two neutrals, and one vibrant. The neutrals serve as a backdrop. For example, my cabinets and counters have grey tones. These items are expensive to replace, so it is smart to select a color that will go with anything. Inside my kitchen cabinets, however, you will see a vibrant burst of teal in the bins I use to store items. Teal is a color I love to use in my home. But, if I fall in love with the color yellow in a year or two, I can easily incorporate a new color into my kitchen by simply changing the bins and buying new kitchen towels.

There are many other ways to personalize and beautify your kitchen. Display beautiful dishes in glass-front cabinets or hang a plant in front of a sunny window to soften the space. Think of ways to incorporate items that are both functional and beautiful: for example, decant dish soap in an attractive dispenser.

CREATE AN EXPERIENCE:
A COFFEE BAR

A coffee bar can be a fun, functional and beautiful space to have in your kitchen, particularly if you like to entertain. Our home coffee bar is a highly-used space, for my own family as well as for visiting friends. It is the first space that welcomes us each morning and the perfect area for a cup of tea and conversation following a delicious evening meal. Setting up a coffee bar is simple, and if you don't have a built-in coffee bar area, you can use a countertop space, or even a bar cart or a small table.

If you are a coffee lover, it is so fun to organize a coffee bar, that perfect place to get that delicious "cuppa" in the morning! The key to organizing an ideal coffee space is to make everything simple to access. Your family and friends should be able to come to the coffee area and easily see everything. The space should ideally be accessible for multiple people at the same time when everyone runs to the coffee bar in the morning.

How to Create a Coffee Bar

My coffee bar is both beautiful and budget-friendly. My kitchen (like many) had a little desk area. However, I didn't utilize this space because it was not functional or necessary for my lifestyle. I believe that you should be willing to reimagine the spaces that take up valuable real estate in your home to get a proper return on investment. To put this belief into practice, I went online and purchased a simple white base cabinet. I added a granite countertop to match the rest of my kitchen countertops. Then, I purchased an old wood china cabinet, a steal at $150. I removed the top portion of the china cabinet (repurposing the bottom part of the cabinet for use in my living room). I painted the top of the china cabinet white and mounted it atop the new base and granite countertop. For a minimal investment, I now had a perfect coffee bar in a previously unused space in my kitchen.

Once you have set up your coffee bar, it's time to stock it! This is the fun part, but you do want to be mindful as you select items for your coffee bar. Think about who will use the space. What do they drink? What items will they need to make it easy to prepare coffee or teas? Most importantly, you want to incorporate all of these items to create a beautiful experience for whoever uses the space.

Tea and Coffee

Because people tend to be either tea or coffee lovers, it's nice to separate these items in your coffee bar. By dividing your coffee and tea items, it's easy for someone to get precisely to what they want, and also simple for you to stock and keep the space in order. I recommend keeping sugar and honey centrally located since they are used with both coffee and tea. It is also nice to designate a place for spoons and napkins that people will need to prepare and enjoy their beverage.

When you select coffee and teas for your coffee bar, consider your own preferences and also try to anticipate what your guests might enjoy. For example, I am a caffeine coffee drinker. I love my caffeine in the morning. But, I do keep decaffeinated coffee stocked in my coffee bar as I have guests who prefer this. I also recommend that you designate specific storage solutions for the coffee and teas, making your offerings easy to identify and minimizing potential clutter. The containers help you to monitor whether you have enough product on hand, help your guests to quickly identify what they need, and finally, they make the space look inviting.

Coffee and Tea Bar Essentials

▶ Tea Box
▶ Coffee Canister
▶ Coffee Spoons
▶ Coffee Cups

▶ Coffee Maker
▶ Coffee Syrups
▶ Cake Plate
▶ Napkins

CHAPTER FOUR

DINING ROOM
The Experience Space

It is so gratifying to me when a client has an "aha" moment in their space. The most simple, straightforward change can have such an impact. I worked with a client who wanted help getting her dining room in order. When I entered the room, I waded into a sea of paperwork. I couldn't even see the top of the table. My client was so overwhelmed that she avoided the room altogether.

As we started to sift through the papers, it was immediately evident to me that the majority could go directly into the recycling bin. However, my client did not feel the same way. Every time I suggested that she purge an item, she gave a reason (or two or three reasons!) why she needed it. Although I disagreed with her reasons, I knew that I needed to take a different approach. For example, my client had a big pile of business cards she had collected over time. Her reason for keeping the cards was to be able to get in touch with the business owner, "just in case." I asked her to think about the time and work it would take to organize the many business cards, and the additional time it would take to find a card if or when she needed it. This time could be spent digging in her garden—something that truly brings her joy—and business contact information could be accessed online in mere seconds. This was the simplest concept, but it was like a lightbulb turned on! We were able to proceed and turn her dining room back into a space to be enjoyed.

When family and friends share their favorite memories of visiting my home, I notice that many of their memories occurred in our dining room. I think this room is memorable because I designed the space to give family and friends a beautiful experience. This is why I like to refer to this area as the "experience space" in my home. Most times it involves food, drinks, and excellent conversation, which is always a recipe for a great time.

STEP ONE: ASSESS YOUR DINING ROOM

The dining room should be a streamlined area in your home. There are certain essential elements for an organized and functional dining room: an area to sit and enjoy a meal and an area to store items necessary to the space.

Think about how you use your dining room. Is it a formal space that is rarely entered, used only on holidays and special occasions? Perhaps your dining area is less

formal and your family uses it multiple times each day. Whether formal or informal, is your dining table a collection point for clutter? If so, why? Are there things you can do or systems you can implement to manage this? Do you need to use your dining area for things other than meals? For example, do you pay bills or work at your dining table? Do your kids do homework at the table?

There are ways to meet your particular needs and to make this space beautifully organized, no matter how you use your dining room.

STEP TWO: *DECLUTTER* YOUR DINING ROOM

The dining room table is often a collection point for a variety of items: school work, mail, even laundry. (Yes, I've seen it—and even done it!) When the dining table is covered in clutter, there is a barrier to being able to use it for its intended purpose: gathering to enjoy a shared meal and conversation.

Decluttering the dining room is usually a matter of purging unneeded items (it's time to deal with that junk mail pile!) and returning misplaced items to their proper places.

STEP THREE: *CLEAN* YOUR DINING ROOM

If used only for meals, the dining area usually requires only a basic cleaning routine to keep the dust clear and the floors clean.

◁ GENERAL CLEANING ▷

Depending on your use of this space, the cleaning process may vary. I find that most dining room cleaning routines are quite simple. A formal dining room may not be used often and will require a quick, weekly once-over; an everyday dining area will obviously need a daily tidying. Typically, you will wipe the table surface and sweep or vacuum under the table as needed.

◁ SPECIALTY CLEANING ▷

Often, a formal dining room houses fine china and silver pieces. Although these pieces do not need to be regularly cleaned, when it *is* time to clean them, the task can feel overwhelming. I find that silver cleaning wipes are the most efficient way to keep silver looking polished and beautiful, a great alternative to messy, smelly creams and liquids.

If you have carpet or a rug in your dining room, you will want to be ready to act quickly to deal with spills and messes. Keep a non-toxic carpet spray with your cleaning supplies so you are prepared when accidents occur!

STEP FOUR: *ORGANIZE* YOUR DINING ROOM

A dining room is typically a straightforward space to organize. When the dining area is used for mealtime—whether everyday meals or a more formal dining space for holidays and special occasions—a dining table and chairs are the essentials. It's also useful to have a furniture piece for storage.

◁ DINING TABLE ▷

The dining table is the centerpiece of the dining room. Your table should be large enough to comfortably seat your immediate family. If you entertain often, you may want a larger table or a table with a leaf to expand as needed. Of course, you may also bring in extra furniture as needed for holidays.

◁ *SEATING* ▷

Ideally, chairs are comfortable enough that people want to linger over dinner and dessert. Cushions can soften hard seating, or you can opt for upholstered dining room chairs. (If you have small children, look for durable upholstered chairs. For example, leather cleans up nicely!)

For extra seating, consider keeping a set of attractive wood folding chairs to use as needed.

◁ *CHINA CABINET OR BUFFET* ▷

Not many of us have a dining room that can accommodate a dining table, china cabinet, *and* a buffet. You must decide what furniture pieces are necessary for your dining room and the way you typically use the space. A dining room buffet offers a great place to organize your serving pieces, dinner napkins, and flatware; it also doubles as a place to set food and drinks to serve. For years, I had a china cabinet in my dining room. Although it was an excellent piece for storage purposes, it did not give me a place to serve food. This is why I now prefer a buffet over a china cabinet.

TIP

It can be expensive to install a custom built-in wall unit in your dining room. A budget-friendly way to achieve a built-in look is to purchase pre-made cabinets and install molding around the cabinets to create an integrated appearance.

AN ENTERTAINING CLOSET

If you frequently entertain (or even if your entertaining is typically around holidays and special occasions), I highly recommend creating an entertaining closet to house various pieces you use when you have guests. As you prepare to organize your entertaining closet, envision your favorite houseware store. We are drawn to beautiful retail spaces with eye-catching arrangements and perfect lighting. These elements attract you to certain shops, and you can create the same effect right in your own home.

◁ HOW TO ORGANIZE AN ENTERTAINING CLOSET ▷

The first step in organizing your entertaining closet is to organize dishware by color. For example, blue plates and green plates should be divided into separate stacks. Next, sort your glassware by type. Finally, separate serving pieces: gold, silver, and so on. This may feel over-the-top, but these divisions are aesthetically pleasing and help you to quickly get to the items you need—beauty *and* function!

Create a "canvas" by arranging the shelving before you place items in the closet. I love white walls and white shelving. Just like an artist, you are creating a masterpiece, and it all starts with a blank canvas. If you are a person who loves neutral colors, you will naturally be drawn to the white walls. If you are a person who loves color, I assure you that white is still a perfect canvas for your entertaining closet; it will make your colorful items pop, giving a beautiful, vibrant look to the space.

When you implement shelving in your entertaining closet space, promise yourself that this space is all you will allow for storage of entertaining pieces. This will help you to avoid purchasing items that are beyond what you have the space to store or that do not coordinate with existing items in the space. If you *do* purchase more than your space can accommodate, you will need to purge something to make room for new items.

The final step is to determine your layout. I recommend placing lighter items (such as glass or white pieces) in the front of the closet nearest to the door to make the space feel open and more extensive. Place colorful items toward the back. Use bins or baskets in a single style and color for a clean, elegant look. These are the perfect place to store small items such as napkins and napkins rings.

Dual-Function Dining Room

Not that long ago, most people thought of the dining room as a formal space used only for special occasions and entertaining guests. Some people (including me!) still think of their dining rooms this way. However, busy modern life means that we may need to rethink the role of the formal dining room in our homes. This space has so much potential to provide us with alternative functions when it is not in use for dining. Remember, you have to determine how to best utilize the spaces in your home so that they function optimally for you and your family. How you use your dining room will determine the best way to organize it to suit your needs.

◁ *SCHOOL WORK* ▷

For school-aged children, the dining room can offer a quiet space to do homework. Or, for families who home-school their children, the dining room can be easily converted to a classroom space during the day and just as easily turned back into a dining space for mealtime. The key is to keep supplies accessible, and to be able to quickly return items to where they belong.

Beautiful file boxes or magazine files can store workbooks, graph paper, and other school supplies. You can use boxes or bins in different colors for each child.

Protect your dining room table from scratches and crayon marks with a vinyl tablecloth. You can even find world map vinyl tablecloths online!

◁ *HOME OFFICE* ▷

The dining room can also double as an office. For years, I used our dining room table as my desk. It provided ample work space; I found clever ways to incorporate beautiful desk accessories to hold my office supplies since the dining room table did not have drawer space. Although I now have a home office, I still love to occasionally sneak away to my dining room for conference calls or when I conduct virtual organizing sessions with clients.

A bar cart is commonly found in the dining room, so it is a perfect piece to use to discreetly store office supplies. Style your cart for office use just as you might for use as an actual bar cart. Use wine glasses (preferably non-transparent) to store paper clips, sticky notes, and other office essentials. A cocktail shaker can be used to store pens and highlighters. A decorative box or a lidded ice bucket can conceal larger items, such as a stapler. The key is to make the bar cart *look* like it is styled for the dining room but *function* like a home office.

A beautiful tote allows you to quickly transition from dining space to workspace. You can conceal work items such as a laptop and files, and easily transport those items as needed.

◁ CRAFTING ▷

A dining room and craft room partnership is high-risk. A dining room should be a beautiful, streamlined space. A craft room, on the other hand, typically houses a wide variety of supplies and tools used for creative projects. Although these spaces are very different at heart, they can work together with the right organization system in place.

Years ago, when we lived in New Jersey, I was obsessed with scrapbooking. At the time, we lived in military housing. The space was extremely small, and I had to make do with the dining table and a crafting bag. A fellow military wife often opened her home for craft nights, transforming her entire downstairs into one big craft room. On these nights, a parade of military spouses would roll their craft bags down the sidewalk; those evenings gave us so many great memories!

It is crucial to purge all craft items down to the must-haves. Once you have pared down to the basics, determine if you would prefer a mobile crafting solution or if you would prefer to house your crafting items in the dining room.

Of course, one downside of a crafter bag is that you have to sift through different compartments to find the items you need. Instead, consider designating a discreet but permanent solution in your dining room so you can more easily enjoy crafting. Organize your materials into different bins that can be stored in or near your dining room for quick access.

◁ GAME NIGHT ▷

A few years ago, I was inspired to create a temporary game room for my family to enjoy playing cards and board games over the holidays. I transformed our dining table into a fantastic game table by covering it with red felt purchased from a fabric store. For a custom look, I simply taped the edges of the fabric under the table. You would have thought you were in Vegas, and it was a hit with my family! The same could be done for an occasional poker or game night.

STEP FIVE: *BEAUTIFY YOUR DINING ROOM*

When I was a child, the dining room was a sacred place. My mother had white carpet and exquisite furniture. It was a "special" room that we rarely entered. It was such a dreamy space in our home. I believe my memories of that room play a huge part in why I love to use white decor in my own house today.

Whether you have a formal dining room, a dining room that functions as a multi-purpose space, or a dining area that accommodates busy daily family life—from breakfast to homework to dinnertime—there are many opportunities to make your dining room a beautiful space for your family and your guests.

TIP

As you organize your dining room, pretend you're an employee at your favorite high-end retail store. This might help you to be more thoughtful about how to arrange your space for both function *and* beauty, and put a bit of fun into a task that might otherwise feel tedious!

Of course, dining room furniture takes center stage in a dining room. Tables and chairs come in all shapes and colors. Depending on your space, you may prefer a more unified, formal look, or a casual (even mismatched) look.

Table linens can dress your table up and add color to the space. Likewise, an area rug under the table can soften the room as well as protect your floors—just make sure the dimensions of the rug are adequate to allow for chairs to be pushed out.

Fresh flowers always look lovely as a table centerpiece. Candles can add warmth and ambiance. A beautiful piece of artwork hung over a dining room buffet can brighten the room and serve as a conversation starter. Beautiful mirrors will reflect light around the space, making the room appear bright and cheerful.

Your dining room can be an amazing, versatile space for your home. Organize and style your space to bring joy to you and your family!

CREATE AN EXPERIENCE
A WINE-TASTING PARTY

Just like wine and cheese, a wine room and dining room are a perfect pairing. The dining room is a perfect space to entertain and enjoy a lovely glass of wine. It's important to organize the space in a manner that allows you to easily serve your guests; of course, it's just as important to create an ambiance to encourage your guests to relax. Your objective is not to store wine (that's for a wine cellar), but rather to facilitate the enjoyment of wine!

◁ WINE DISPLAY ▷

There are many ways to beautifully and creatively display the wine you will serve. For example, a beautiful wine rack or serving tray adds an element of elegance. You could also use a bar cart to hold the wine you will serve.

Consider creating a menu of the various wines with the type of wine, country of origin, winery, and year, along with a description of the wine. You can serve cheese, fruit, or chocolate to pair with the wines.

◁ WINE COLLECTIONS ▷

You can educate and entertain your guests at the same time! Categorize the wines by region or type. You could even include interesting facts about the wineries you are featuring.

TIP

Keep red wine stain remover handy in case of accidental spills.

◁ WINE GLASSES ▷

Consider the various types of wine glasses you will need. Wine glasses are naturally delicate and elegant and will enhance your decor. You also want to think about how much space is required for your wine glasses, and how you will display them.

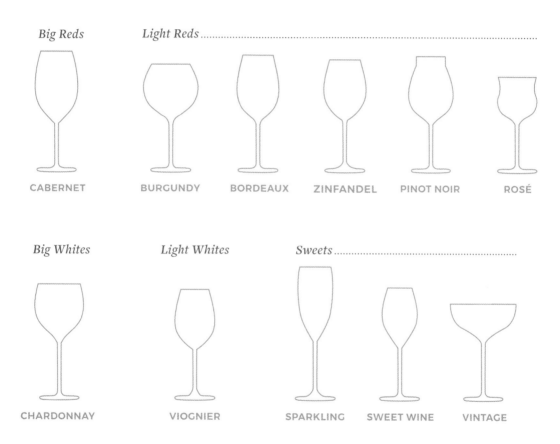

Big Reds   *Light Reds* ....

CABERNET   BURGUNDY   BORDEAUX   ZINFANDEL   PINOT NOIR   ROSÉ

Big Whites   *Light Whites*   *Sweets* ....

CHARDONNAY   VIOGNIER   SPARKLING   SWEET WINE   VINTAGE

CHAPTER FIVE

LIVING & FAMILY ROOMS
The Gathering Spaces

One client I worked with had an unfortunate habit of buying additional furniture every time she needed to store items in her tiny living room space. Because her home was small, my client needed to utilize this room to house a wide variety of items such as serving dishes, books, linens, and home office essentials. However, if the number of books she owned suddenly exceeded the space, she would just buy another cabinet. When her piles of paperwork and collection of stationery grew, she would add another desk. The room was crammed with furniture that completely overwhelmed the space. My client longed for a beautifully organized living room. Luckily, beauty and organization just happen to be my areas of expertise!

I asked my client to try to think of her belongings as accessories, items to make her home feel elegant and beautiful. We kept only one of my client's three cabinets: selecting a substantial glass-front piece to showcase in her living room. We selected her most attractive books, serving dishes, and linens, and styled them carefully. We layered items to use space effectively, stacking white serving bowls on top of each other and draping colorful linen napkins over the sides of the bowls. We arranged and stacked her books by color to give the cabinet a clean look. Our goal was to create a beautiful visual display. My client had so much fun creating vignettes in her cabinet that her frustration completely disappeared.

I was so happy to see my client fall in love with her space again; it was truly a professional organizer's dream come true. This client's key to success was to realize that her necessary items were beautiful, and that they could also serve as home décor accessories. When items can play double-duty in this way, you can efficiently and attractively display and feature the things that you truly love.

Some homes have both a living room and a family room; others have only one of these spaces. Regardless, every home needs a gathering space where everyone can kick back. These spaces should be beautiful and promote relaxation. Living rooms and family rooms are spaces to kick back and gather together, places to do homework, play games, or to simply enjoy conversation.

STEP ONE: ASSESS YOUR LIVING ROOM

As you consider your living or family room space, think about how your family uses the room. What activities do you like to do together? What makes you feel truly at home, like you can put your feet up and relax? Are there items—games or books—that you like to have on hand to promote a feeling of togetherness in your gathering space? What about items to promote comfort and relaxation?

Consider the furniture in your living room. Do you have adequate seating for the number of people who typically use the space? Do you have coffee or side tables placed conveniently for resting a beverage or playing a board game? Perhaps you have too much furniture, which can make a room feel cramped. Assess your living or family room space with a critical eye, thinking about how you can enhance the elements that are conducive to how you use the space, as well as how you might eliminate elements that prevent you from using the space in the way you wish.

STEP TWO: DECLUTTER YOUR LIVING ROOM

If your living room is a gathering place for the members of your family, it may also be a gathering place for clutter! Magazine, video game controllers, half-finished school reports—it can all land in the living room. As you begin to declutter, first focus on returning items that do not belong to their proper places. Once you have done this, look deeper. Anything that does not serve a purpose—either in the living room or elsewhere in your home—should be thrown away or donated.

◁ MEDIA ▷

Do you have a large DVD collection? Rather than storing DVDs in bulky cases, consider buying compact, zippered cases to store your DVDs.

◁ BOOKS ▷

Many people love to collect books, but they do take up a lot of space. If you have a book collection, take the time to sort through your stacks; donate any books that you won't read again (or ones that you haven't ever gotten around to reading!).

◁ ELECTRONICS ▷

Many families have at least one "gamer" among them. Devices, controllers, and games take up a lot of space, and cords have a way of snaking across the living room floor. Eliminate unused games or accessories from the space.

STEP THREE: *CLEAN YOUR LIVING ROOM*

After you have decluttered, thoroughly clean your living room. Dust the blinds, vacuum behind furniture and beneath sofa cushions. Remove items and dust shelves; you can even go the extra mile and have the rugs shampooed! It may be a big job but know that the coziness and your enjoyment of your living room will be enhanced once it has been spruced up.

STEP FOUR: *ORGANIZE YOUR LIVING ROOM*

The living room is a place to relax and a place to come together to enjoy the company of the people you care about. Organize your living room to make the time you spend with your loved ones memorable.

◁ *GAMES* ▷

In my family, board games are a big part of the fun. We have a variety of favorite games we like to play together. I love that there are so many attractive board games on the market today. I grew up playing Scrabble® and Monopoly®, and I am delighted by the elegant "book style" versions of these games. They look great on a family room bookshelf. Card games can also be stored on a bookshelf in an attractive basket, box, or bin. Finally, there are many classy options for coffee table games. Consider a beautiful chess set, for example.

I also keep crossword puzzle books on the coffee table. Even though this is a quiet, individual game, it's still lovely to sit around and chat while we are engaged in our own activities. However, games on phones do not seem to follow the same pattern. I notice that any activity on a mobile phone tends to distract and isolate people. Perhaps this is why I feel so strongly about physical games as a way to connect with the people whom I love.

Games of all kinds can bring you together with the people you care about and add elements of beauty and fun to a family or living room space!

◁ *COFFEE TABLE ORGANIZATION* ▷

A coffee table is often a central piece of furniture in a living or family room space. It is a functional piece, a place to play games or to set a drink. Most important, the coffee table anchors the room and is a central point around which family and friends gather. As such, your coffee table should be selected with care.

FAMILY PHOTO ORGANIZATION

My family loves to sit in the living room and look through old family photos together. In this digital age, it is becoming rare to find traditional photo books on family room shelves. While digital photos are certainly a convenient way to store photos, I still feel that there is something so special about sitting around the living room with my family, flipping through old family albums. This provokes beautiful conversations; we put down our phones and truly engage with each other. Physical photographs possess almost tangible memories and a feeling of love that is impossible to get from a digital photo. Even though albums take up valuable space in my home, I wouldn't have it any other way. However, it is still smart to digitize photos and back them up to the cloud or to a storage device.

There are a number of ways to organize family photos. Most digital photo storage options allow you to "tag" photographs in any way you deem useful. Here are some ways to organize photos:

By Family Member
Create an album or albums that span a given family member's life. This method is special because it dedicates albums to a particular person. When organized in this manner, the albums also become treasured items to pass down to children or grandchildren.

By Event
You can also choose to organize photos by event. Weddings, family vacations, and other special events can be documented in an album dedicated specifically to that event. These albums essentially highlight a timeline of special events in your family history.

Printed Photo Books
If you already store your photos digitally, there are many services that make it simple to create custom photo books that feature your digital photos. If this seems daunting, there are even services that create a photo book for you! This option may be the best of both worlds, as it allows you to keep your digital photos and curate your favorite images to include in a physical book. Further, you can easily order multiple copies of the same book to share with other family members.

Digital Photo Storage
Digital photo storage is great on a number of levels: it takes no physical space and allows you to preserve photographs that might otherwise get damaged or

deteriorate with time. Digitizing photos also makes it easy to share treasured photos with other members of your family.

In the age of social media, we often document our lives on the go. It's wonderful to view these photos as a history of your daily life. Whether you are cataloging already-digitized photos or scanning and preserving older photos, it can be a a laborious and time-consuming process to digitally organize your photos. I recommend that you create a schedule to get your photos in order. For example, you may commit to organizing photos to create one digital album a month. The key is to make progress on the task instead of becoming overwhelmed and procrastinating. However, if you are overwhelmed, there are services that can tackle this sort of project for you!

I love a coffee table that is a conversation piece in itself. There are many interesting and lovely coffee tables on the market. I actually created my coffee table myself out of an array of picture frames. It is a fun addition to the space and it's a great conversation starter that always gets friends and family talking. This simple project brings so much function and beauty to my living room and makes the space unique to me. I encourage you to find ways to make your home uniquely yours!

I recommend that you keep your coffee table neat and minimal. Placing too many items on the table creates a feeling of clutter. Plus, the more you have on the table, the more there is to clean! There are, however, a few types of attractive items that enhance a coffee table:

Coffee Table Books

Coffee table books are both beautiful and interesting, great additions to any living or family room space. A great coffee table book is visually appealing and introduces something new. I try to choose coffee table books with a wide variety of subjects. A budget-friendly way to incorporate coffee table books into your space is to use your local library. Check out unusual books on compelling subjects; you can continually rotate your coffee table book selections!

Coasters

Coasters are necessary to protect your table. Keep coasters in plain view on your coffee table surface to remind family and friends to use them. If you prefer a stream-lined coffee table look, you can opt to store your coasters in a beautiful box on a nearby shelf or cabinet and pull them out when drinks will be enjoyed in the space. Another option is to stock cocktail napkins on a bar cart in the living or family room space.

Storage

A coffee table may also offer storage. Utilize the space beneath your coffee table; incorporate beautiful baskets or bins so you can easily tuck away toys, books, or blankets that can be pulled out to cuddle around the fireplace.

◁ BEVERAGE CART ▷

A bar cart is a wonderful addition to any living space. It is an ideal piece to beautifully arrange and use to welcome your guests. I love bar carts for their versatility; you can customize a bar cart to meet a variety of needs beyond mixing the perfect cocktail. Bar carts are also very beneficial in small places because they are both compact and mobile. There are so many ways to creatively use a bar cart:

Cocktail Cart

Obviously, a bar cart is most often used to mix drinks. If you choose to use your bar cart for its traditional use, consider making it user-friendly by providing miniature liquor bottles so that guests can easily create their favorite beverage.

Water Cart

A bar cart can serve as a perfect water station on a hot day. If I am expecting guests and the temperature is climbing, I set out bottled water, glasses, a bowl of lemon slices, straws, and cocktail napkins. Another option is to fill a beautiful beverage dispenser with flavored ice water. Of course, you should add a bit of decor—a vase of flowers or a potted succulent, perhaps—along with the essentials to create a beautiful vignette.

Homework Station

Use your bar cart to create a fun homework station for kids. You can serve after-school snacks and beverages from the tray. You can also incorporate homework supplies such as pencils, flashcards, and paper. Consider stocking bright, patterned pencils or fun paper straws to make the cart attractive to kids. Place the homework station near wherever your kids typically do their homework, and the cart becomes a pleasant gathering point. For working parents whose children may arrive home first, the homework station cart might even be a way to connect with your children and make them feel special each day.

STEP FIVE: *BEAUTIFY* YOUR LIVING ROOM

Living and family rooms are spaces where we entertain or simply where we relax. Music, lighting, and comfort items can be incorporated into the space to create a warm atmosphere—but it's important to take care that these things do not create unnecessary clutter.

◁ *MUSIC* ▷

Music can set the mood in your home. It can be our motivator at cleaning time, bring in the sound of the holidays, or create a festive vibe when you entertain guests. If you don't want to install an expensive sound system, you can use a speaker light bulb (also known as a smart bulb); you will be able to use your smartphone to play music from your living room lamp!

◁ *LIGHTING* ▷

Lighting helps to set the tone of a space. Notice the color of your light bulbs; the right color makes a big difference in creating ambience. Light bulbs can be a warm white or soft white, emitting a yellow or warm light, or daylight which will emit a cooler light. To achieve the perfect light color, read the lighting facts on the light bulb packaging to find your desired temperature, from warm to cool.

◁ *COMFORT* ▷

There are many options to create a cozy feeling *and* enhance your decor; blankets can be incorporated in a variety of ways. Toss a throw blanket casually over the arm of the sofa, roll a blanket and place it in a beautiful basket near the fireplace, or fold a few blankets and stack them neatly on a bookcase shelf or in a cabinet. Throw pillows and candles can also elevate the feeling of coziness in the living room.

Domino

However, comfort isn't just about textiles. In a room that is meant for family, you might choose to display personal photographs of family members in beautiful frames. You can also incorporate keepsakes and other meaningful pieces such as artwork into your décor as a way to infuse the space with your own unique personality.

CREATE AN EXPERIENCE FAMILY FUN NIGHT

While it could be argued that *every* night can be special, why not go the extra mile to create an experience—and memories—for your family.

◁ COFFEE TABLE FUN ▷

I love to keep a game such as tic-tac-toe on the coffee table. Such a simple item can create instant fun and a way for family and friends to connect. Games like these come in all sorts of beautiful forms such as glass, wood, or marble. There's something to fit any décor style!

◁ FAMILY FUN NIGHT ▷

Get creative and use your bar cart to promote family fun at home. Include a bowl of popcorn, beverages, and board games on the cart and gather your family in the living or family room. Get creative: try a banana split bar or a s'mores station!

◁ CANDY BAR ▷

Who loves a great candy bar? I sure do! While it's probably not a good idea to have a candy-stocked bar cart in your home year-round, it's a fun option for special times such as Christmas, or the end of the school year. You can even stock a candy bar for the next baby shower or birthday party you host! To create a candy bar cart, simply fill a variety of jars and bowls with delicious candy. Tiered trays are also an attractive way to display candy.

There are an endless number of ways to get creative to make special experiences for your loved ones. Have a classic movie night, a cozy family reading night, or even a family dance party (a favorite for little kids).

CHAPTER SIX

HOME OFFICE
The Management Space

P aperwork gets the best of, well, the best of us. It can feel like a constant battle to stay on top of statements, records, and other pertinent documents. Paperwork continually trickles into the house, and we are left to cram it into filing cabinets or to pile it on ever-higher stacks. Or are we?

I love to help people organize their home files. One client I worked with had a large, two-drawer filing cabinet. It was stuffed with all kinds of papers, and she had another large pile in the corner of her bedroom. When I told her that we were going to reduce the paperwork to a quarter of what she currently had, she looked at me with disbelief.

This particular client had formed a habit of filing everything—at least until she ran out of space. For example, she had a file for every type of utility service. In these utility files, she had accumulated years' worth of monthly statements. As we worked together, she realized that she took time to file the statements each month, but that she never had reason to reference those statements. We simplified her system: she kept only her account numbers and service agreements in a single "Utilities" file and switched to electronic billing for her monthly statements. We approached the rest of her files similarly, significantly paring back her paperwork to keep only the essentials. When our task was complete, my client felt empowered to stay on top of her bills and other paperwork and she loved that her bedroom now felt like a place to retreat and rest, rather than like an untidy office.

———◇———

I believe that every home—big or small—should have a home office. This may be a grand space with French doors and elegant built-in bookcases. It may be a closet that has been creatively transformed into a work space or a desk tucked in a quiet corner. If space is lacking, your "home office" may even be a mobile affair, such as a rolling case that can be tucked under the bed or in a closet and accessed when you need it. This chapter will guide you to create systems to set up and maintain a beautifully organized home office space that suits your family's needs.

STEP ONE: ASSESS YOUR HOME OFFICE

Since a home office is not often considered a "must have" room such as a bathroom or kitchen, it may be overlooked as a space that needs to be thoughtfully organized. A home office can be a convenient space in which to efficiently handle home matters and finances, or even a necessary space if you work from home. For home use, you need a place to store files to easily reference as needed. Ideally, you should also have a secure place to store documents such as passports, medical documents, and financial records.

Do you already have a dedicated home office area? If so, does the space adequately provide for your needs? For example, if you work at home, you may need more space than if you only use your office to pay bills once a month. Many people also need their home office spaces to have dual-function—for example, to double as a guest bedroom. Is this true for you?

Do you have a system in place for paperwork? Or rather, do you have *systems* in place? You will need a place in which to organize your existing files *and* you need a way to quickly and efficiently handle new paperwork that enters your home. (Don't worry, we'll talk more about this later in the chapter.)

A home office is a functional space; having the proper furnishings in place will allow your office to work as you need it to. Remember, though: home office furniture can be both functional *and* beautiful. In fact, choosing attractive furniture pieces will make your home office feel more like an integrated part of your home. You may even find that you enjoy the time spent at your desk! The following furniture items are typically found in home office areas; what do you need for your space?

◁ DESK ▷

Of course, a desk is a key component of the home office space. When you choose a desk for your office, consider function, comfort, and beauty. Does the desk have adequate drawer space? Is the work surface large enough for your needs? Is the scale of the desk appropriate for the space it will go; is it also appropriately sized for your body? Don't underestimate the importance of having an aesthetically pleasing desk. After all, you want the time you spend at the desk to be as enjoyable as possible, even if you are paying bills!

◁ SEATING ▷

If you work at home and spend a significant amount of time at your desk, it is worth investing in an ergonomic desk chair. This will save your back in the long run! Thankfully, there are attractive ergonomic chairs on the market. These chairs can be expensive; I recommend trying out chairs at the store before you commit to purchasing one.

I also like to keep a comfortable armchair in my home office. If I have something lengthy to read, I enjoy curling up in my armchair rather than sitting at my desk.

◁ *BOOKCASE* ▷

A bookcase may or may not be an item you need in your home. Some people prefer to keep novels in the den or to use attractive hardcover books as home décor. However, if you have a collection of books that you reference in your work, these may be better placed in your home office.

◁ *FILING CABINET* ▷

You will need a place to store files. You may require an actual filing cabinet, but you may also be able to use a smaller file storage box. Before you rush to purchase a new piece for file storage, make sure you declutter and organize your paperwork to better understand what file storage solution you need.

◁ *SAFE* ▷

If you do not use a bank safety deposit box for vital records, identification documents (like passports and birth certificates), or expensive jewelry, consider investing in a fireproof home office safe. Choose a model that can be bolted to the ground for added security.

STEP TWO: *DECLUTTER* YOUR HOME OFFICE

As a professional organizer, I find that clients tend to keep way more paperwork than is strictly necessary. Home offices can sometimes be easily closed off from the rest of the home; it can be tempting to allow papers and all manner of items to pile up there. Unfortunately, many home offices become a paper-infested dumping ground and it can be difficult to be focused and productive in a cluttered space. This usually happens when organization systems are lacking.

To begin getting your office area in order, follow the decluttering method that I shared in chapter one. Remove items that belong elsewhere. Shred or recycle excess paperwork. (This process may be repeated as you continue to refine your home office organization.) Throw away broken staplers and pens that are out of ink. Do you have a broken printer sitting in the corner, a fax machine that hasn't seen action since the late 1990s, or a stash of old cell phones? Find an electronics recycling facility and get rid of these items! Only with a realistic view of the space and the items that belong there will you be able to assess the storage solutions you will need.

STEP THREE: *CLEAN* YOUR HOME OFFICE

In addition to acting as a collection point for paperwork and other clutter, the home office also tends to collect dust! Once you have decluttered but before you begin to organize, take the time to thoroughly clean your office area and all the furniture in it. Wipe out desk and file cabinet drawers. Dust bookshelves and vacuum the floor, taking care to get behind furniture and along baseboards.

◁ *DAILY TIDYING* ▷

Although I don't enjoy most cleaning, I do enjoy tidying my home office, perhaps because it is a space that is uniquely mine. When you prepare to leave your home office, take a moment to straighten your desk. This helps prevent an accumulation of clutter, and it is pleasant to sit down at a neat desk.

◁ *SPECIALTY CLEANING ITEMS* ▷

I generally like to keep the number of cleaning products I have on hand to a minimum, but there are a few specialty products that are useful for the home office. Keep an air can to clean your computer keyboard, and special wipes or a microfiber cloth to keep your screen clean. You might consider creating a mini cleaning caddy to keep in an office desk drawer.

STEP FOUR: *ORGANIZE* YOUR HOME OFFICE

As with other spaces in the home, I recommend that you curate your home office to include items that are truly useful.

◁ *SUPPLIES* ▷

Keep only essential office supplies on hand. For most people, it is sufficient to have a few pens, a stapler, and a pair of scissors. Office supplies can be tucked away in a drawer, or there are many stylish desktop storage solutions to keep your desktop from becoming an eyesore.

◁ *ACTION BOX* ▷

A desktop "Action Box" is useful for items that require your attention. This may be household bills that need to be paid, or a child's field trip permission form. However, to prevent a pile-up of paper in the action box, the key to success is to assign a deadline to the box. Pick one weekly "deadline" day: this is the day that you commit to clearing all items from your Action Box. If you deal with a large amount of paper and forms on a weekly basis, you might consider using binder clips labeled with each day of the week. You can then easily clip an item by the day that you need to handle it.

◁ HOME FILES ▷

A home office space is an ideal place to address the various matters that need attention in daily life, but it can also be a place to implement a filing system for important documents. Every home needs some filing system in place. Whether you are eighteen years old and living in your first apartment or forty years old and purchasing your dream home, you need a place and method to organize important documents that relate to your family and home. Some people will need filing systems for their business as well. The type of filing system you choose depends on how you work and how you choose to maintain your records.

Home File Organization Methods

The first thing to do as you start to organize your home files is decide what system you want to use to maintain your records. Here are methods I find to be useful for home file organization:

TRADITIONAL FILING A traditional filing method is one in which you label a folder with a category, insert the documents pertaining to that category in the folder, and store it in a file cabinet. There are a variety of efficient filing tools on the market to help you to maintain your home files.

BINDER SYSTEM The binder system is my preferred method to keep home files; it is the system I use in my own home. I have one three-ring binder specific to each category of information that we maintain. I like this system because our files are both easily accessible and portable; it is easy to take a binder with me if I need to handle business away from home. When we lived in the United Kingdom years ago, I worked as a registrar at an elementary school. The school used the binder system to maintain records for all of the students. At first, I thought it was crazy to use binders instead of file folders. But, after working with this system for several years, I was sold. I found that it was the most efficient way to keep up with so much information. When my family moved back to the United States, I adapted and implemented a binder system for our home files and I have loved it ever since.

If you are young and have relatively few files to maintain, you might be able to start with just one binder. However, as you go through life, you can expand your binder system as needed.

GO PAPERLESS In today's digital world, a paperless filing system is a reasonable thing to consider. Most business is transacted online, so most invoices, receipts, and other documents are provided electronically, making it simple to keep a paperless system. There are also a number of streamlined, easy-to-use scanners on the market that you can use to make digital copies of paper documents. I love the fact that with a paperless system, you can access your files anytime, anywhere.

If you opt for a paperless system, you still need to set it up so that it is easy and efficient to use. You should create specific electronic files for each category pertaining to your home and life so that you can quickly locate the items you need.

Not everyone is computer-savvy; in fact, technology can be frustrating to some people. Choose a system you are comfortable with and you will be more likely to use and maintain it.

Home File Categories

The following categories are fitting for most households. If you are lost when it comes to how to organize your files, you might find this list helpful. Of course, you can adapt these categories to fit your life, family, and home needs. Remember: keep only what is essential!

AUTOMOBILE The automobile file is for records that relate to your vehicle(s) such as loan agreements or title documents. Some people like to keep car maintenance records, but I find that doing so quickly generates paper clutter. If you always have your car serviced at the same place, the service provider will likely keep electronic records in your name.

BANKING Keep bank account numbers on file but take care to secure this information. (There are a number of reputable apps that allow you to securely store account numbers and passwords.) I refrain from keeping physical bank statements, as these can be easily found online if needed.

I also keep one current checkbook in this file. Checkbooks can be bulky, so additional checks may be kept in a desk drawer, in your safe, or in the back of a file cabinet.

CHARITY Keep a file for all charitable contributions. This may include church tithing records, donation statements, and receipts from charitable donations made throughout the year. It's also a good idea to keep a record of the tax ID numbers for organizations to which you contribute. At tax time, you will be thankful that you kept such tidy records!

CHURCH My family keeps a church binder; this is the home for our baptism records, church membership information, and so forth. We do, however, keep our church financial records in our charity binder, as this is most useful to us at tax time.

CREDIT CARD STATEMENTS Credit card statements are easily accessed via your online account and it is cumbersome to keep many months' worth of paper statements. However, I do keep the most current statement on file in physical form. If a fraudulent charge appears, it is useful to have a hard copy at my fingertips.

HOME MAINTENANCE I like to record when we have our home serviced for a variety of reasons: gutter cleaning, HVAC service, and so on. If something goes wrong, it's useful to have these records for warranty or claim purposes. If you plan to sell the property at some point in the future, it can also be very useful to show that you have maintained and/or improved the home during the time you owned it.

INSURANCE POLICIES Keep insurance policies on file so they can be quickly and easily referenced, including homeowner, life, and automobile insurance.

Review your insurance annually for gaps in coverage and to make sure your policies reflect your current needs and provide the protection you need.

INVESTMENT RECORDS This file is for 401k, pension, and other pertinent retirement plan information. These documents concern your future; it's very important to keep statements and other correspondence you receive regarding your retirement accounts and any other investments you may have. I recommend scanning the documents you receive yearly; keep an electronic file organized by year.

LOAN DOCUMENTS For any loans other than a mortgage, it is important to keep the contracts and policies for reference purposes. If you are able to access statements online, I recommend keeping only the most current statement on file. If you have given a friend or family member a personal loan, keep these records along with payment receipts until the loan has been repaid in full. For any loan that has been fully paid, scan the related documents to reduce your paper clutter.

MEDICAL RECORDS We like to keep our medical records on file, including the childhood medical records for our adult children. As a military family, we have lived several places and have been to several different hospitals. I quickly learned to keep copies of medical records, and even to bring these files when visiting a new physician for the first time. You can certainly request electronic copies of your records from your doctor or hospitals, too.

MONTHLY BILLS Our monthly bill file holds a copy of our budget spreadsheet for the month. My husband and I like to review our budget together over a nice cup of coffee (or a glass of wine depending on how the budget looks!). We keep an electronic spreadsheet, but we also find it useful to look at a printed copy together. We also put incoming bills in this file as they arrive.

PERSONAL HOME INVENTORY Document the items you own. An accurate inventory of your possessions will give you peace of mind if you need to file a claim. My best advice is to use a camera and walk around your home to film all of your possessions.

For big-ticket items like furniture, electronics, jewelry, and so forth, keep track of the date of purchase and purchase price. Keep repair records and appraisals in this file; it is also a good idea to keep receipts for major purchases. While all of this information can be kept in your personal home inventory file, you should also keep an extra copy in a fireproof safe or box, or with someone you trust.

PET RECORDS Pets are wonderful, considered by many people (including me!) to be a true a member of the family. It is important to keep their records in order, too. See page 218 for more information about vital information to keep handy for your pets.

REAL ESTATE Keep real estate documents on file; this might include your rental agreement if you are a renter or mortgage documents if you are a homeowner. (I also keep records for homes we have owned in the past.) Keep titles here or in your safety deposit box. If you own rental properties, you may also want to keep tenant agreements here. It's also useful to keep property tax and appraisal records. Finally, keep spare keys for current real estate in this file.

RECEIPTS Receipts are pesky pieces of paper that clutter handbags, cars, and homes. I am amazed by the amount of paper we use to print receipts. In my home, we scan our important receipts. This is my husband's responsibility. Since I do most of the shopping for our household, I make sure that I put all receipts in their appropriate boxes so that they can be scanned. We have two boxes on the bookcase in our home office: one for home receipts and one for business receipts. I only need to place a receipt in the appropriate box and my job is done. Our system is simple and most importantly, it works well for us.

SCHOOL A "school" file holds copies of all degrees, diplomas, and school transcripts for every member of the family. Anything else school-related goes into this binder, too. If you are currently repaying student loans, monthly statements should go into your monthly bills binder; however, once the loan is paid in full, your loan documentation can be moved to this file or scanned and stored electronically.

If you have school-aged children, I recommend keeping a "parent school binder." See pages 127–128 for more on how to create this useful tool.

TAX DOCUMENTS Your tax file will be one of the most useful files you maintain. This is where you keep all relevant tax items for the current year. I also find it helpful to keep a log that allows me to track what tax documents we need to obtain prior to filing our taxes. When W-2s and other tax documents arrive, they should be immediately placed in this file. I mark off the documents on my log as I file them. When it's time to meet with our accountant each spring, it's easy to grab this file.

Ask your tax advisor what he or she recommends for how many years of taxes to keep on file. I have binders for a ten-year period, with each binder labeled by year. I place completed taxes in the appropriate binder and store them in our bottom file cabinet drawer.

USER MANUALS Most homes will have appliances and other items with accompanying user manuals. These manuals can be bulky and aren't ideal for filing away in a cabinet. Most manuals can be found online, so there isn't always a need to keep paper manuals. You can even keep a folder on your computer for downloaded manuals. If you do keep paper manuals, an attractive magazine holder is a great storage option.

UTILITIES We pay most of our bills online, so I like to minimize paper clutter in the "utilities" binder by only keeping the initial documents from when we established service, and a document that includes pertinent account information. I also like to keep an issue tracker, a simple log where I track maintenance or issues we have with utilities. The tracker is helpful when we make decisions to transfer or change our service, as we can clearly see documented issues. Any paperwork related to billing is kept in our monthly bills binder.

VITAL RECORDS Vital records such as birth certificates, marriage licenses, and death certificates should be kept in a safe, secure place. I keep copies of these documents in our file cabinet to provide to family members as needed. (I even keep copies on hand for my grown children, which they have appreciated on more than one occasion!) I keep the original versions of these documents in a fireproof safe, alongside our passports.

WARRANTIES Keep track of all warranties for any home and personal items. I also keep rebate stubs in this file if I am still awaiting the funds. Once we receive rebate checks, I remove the information from the file.

WILLS I have heard so many stories about the heart-wrenching, messy aftermath of the loss of loved ones when the affairs of the deceased were not in order. It can be difficult to grieve if you are trying to sort through the finances and personal effects of the deceased. Relationships can even be damaged. We do not want this for our families or ourselves during a time of bereavement.

My husband and I keep copies of our own wills on file, as well as copies of wills for other family members whose affairs we will be responsible for in the event of illness or their passing. Once a year, I sit down with my own parents to discuss any updates to wills and living wills. I have heard many friends say they cannot have these types of conversations with their families. No matter how difficult the conversations may be, it's so important to have the security to know that everything is in order, and that wishes can be appropriately carried out. This is particularly important if you have young children of your own!

WORK A "work" file holds resumes, performance appraisals, and work-related certifications that you might need to reference for purposes such as job hunting or when seeking a promotion. As a military spouse, I was often in job search mode because of our frequent moves. My own "work" file was very important to me during these times.

Once you have set up your file system, the key to success is to remember that your goal is to file only essential items. Don't waste time filing and holding on to documents that will never serve a purpose. Treat filing as a quick daily or weekly chore. Do an annual audit of your files and purge any outdated items.

If you know me, you know that I love my planner; I call it my "personal assistant." Technology is taking over the world, but I still believe that there is nothing better than a piece of paper and a beautiful pen to help keep me on task.

In fact, planning is a huge trend. While I love a physical planner, there are many wonderful apps to assist you with planning every aspect of your life. You can use these apps alone or to complement your physical planner. There are many options to assist you in your planning; it simply takes a bit of thought and perhaps some trial and error to discover what will work for you! First, determine the best tools to help you accomplish your mission of organizing your life. Here are some tools to consider:

Electronic Planners

Microsoft Outlook® and Google® (among others) offer calendar features that work seamlessly between your computer, phone, and other devices. Research different planning apps. Read the reviews and try one that sparks your interest. Many apps are free, or at least offer a free trial. As with anything new, give yourself a minimum of two weeks with the app to truly see if it works for you.

Binder or Notebook Planners

Do you prefer a beautiful binder option? I love my three-ring leather planner. Consider the size of the planner you choose; make sure it is substantial enough to allow space to keep track of your personal life (and your work life if necessary). Some people prefer smaller, compact planners that can be easily tucked into a purse or tote. Also consider

the features you will need to help keep your life in order. Some planners only include a calendar; others include space to create lists, track fitness goals, or to manage a budget. Once you have identified the features you require and the size you prefer, you can shop for a planner to meet your needs. One word of caution: there are many planners on the market, and some can be quite expensive. I encourage you not to invest in an expensive planner until you know it is an organizing solution that will work well for you. It might make sense to "trial run" an inexpensive planner first!

Once you have your beautiful new planner, begin by noting the areas in your life that need attention on a daily, weekly, and monthly basis: appointments, home maintenance, work events, and other pertinent items. Most of us balance a host of responsibilities; daily life can feel overwhelming. While a good planner can't actually take on these responsibilities, a planner *can* organize everything in one space. I find that the simple act of writing down an appointment or a to-do item in my planner relieves my brain, reduces any feeling of stress I may have, and brings me a sense of calm. Further, the act of marking off a completed task from my to-do list gives me a huge sense of accomplishment during the day. Let's be real: we are not always going to meal plan each week, meet every work deadline, or hit the gym exactly as planned. It's okay; we're human. However, a planner can help you to regroup and keep you on top of what needs to be done.

I encourage you to make planning a pleasurable experience. I love to add features such as gold metallic priority tabs to my planner so that I can quickly navigate to my daily tasks. I also add accessories such as a pen and tassel. These seemingly small items enhance my planner so that it is unique and special to me.

For successful planning, I believe it's essential to set time aside each week to plan out the following week. I like to do this while watching one of my favorite television shows. Setting a routine will build your relationship with your planner so that you will consistently use it. And of course, this will be a weekly opportunity to list your many responsibilities in your planner, rather than leaving them to rattle around in your head!

STEP FIVE: *BEAUTIFY* YOUR HOME OFFICE

A home office equals work—there's no way around that. Whether you use this space to pay bills, to plan meals, to track appointments, or for your paid employment, you will probably spend a significant amount of time at your desk. It can, however, be a pleasure to sit down in a beautiful home office space. It can even feel like a retreat from the hustle and bustle of the rest of your home! Give thought to items that can make your home office feel like an extension of the rest of your home. Bring beauty to the space with furnishings and accessories that appeal to you.

◁ *LAMP* ▷

A beautiful lamp with soft lighting will immediately create ambiance. Even if your desk is a mess, the soft glow of the lamp will add a positive feeling.

◁ *PLANT LIFE* ▷

Consider adding flowers or a plant to add beauty and life to your desktop. This generates a feeling of life and growth in the space and will perhaps inspire you. A simple potted plant also helps your home office area to blend with the rest of your home. It shows that thought and attention have been given to your space.

◁ *ACCESSORIES* ▷

You do not want your home office to look like the DMV! Purchase attractive desk accessories rather than standard issue office supplies! In addition to a stapler, scissors, and other desktop accessories, you can bring in other items to beautify your space:

Motivational Artwork

Artwork that features a motivational saying can be a fun addition to a home office. You can find pieces in a variety of styles to coordinate with your office space and the rest of your home. A small but subtle piece can provide inspiration and motivation when you need it most!

Candles

A beautiful candle in a stress-relieving scent like lavender can be a lovely addition to your home office.

◁ *MINI REFRESHMENT CENTER* ▷

Consider incorporating a mini refreshment center in a desk drawer. Keep bottled sparkling water, or even tiny bottles of liquor for a cocktail! You might also buy yourself a box of delicious chocolates. Sneak away to your office to enjoy one piece as a special, self-indulgent moment in your day. You deserve it!

TIP

To keep paperwork on your desk beautifully tidy, cut a decorative folder to 8½ x 11 inches, then place the decorative cover over the top of paperwork in your action tray.

Ultimately, your home office should function well, but it should also feel like an extension of the rest of your home, a space to enjoy—even if you are working!

CREATE A PARENT-SCHOOL BINDER

Parents today have so many responsibilities and details to manage, especially when it comes to their children's education. There are many things to do and to remember each and every day. It can be very helpful to have an organization system to help stay on top of school matters. Take some of the pressure off yourself and let the binder do the work! Then you can sit back and shine as a parent.

Years ago, I developed a parent school binder and it worked perfectly to help me stay on top of my son's education. It showed him (and his teachers!) that I was aware of pertinent information. A single binder can be used for multiple children. I recommend keeping the following information and items in your parent school binder:

SCHOOL CALENDAR

The first item to place in your parent school binder is a blank academic calendar. You might want to record key dates (holidays, parent-teacher conferences) in the calendar. Integrate the school and lunch calendars, or keep them as separate documents in the binder. Jot events on the calendar as you become aware of them. In addition to vacation days and school events, consider recording the following information:

Test Dates

Note the date of your child's tests, but also make a quick note on the calendar to inquire about the test grade a few days later. This shows your child that you are engaged in their education and keeping up with how things are going.

Sick Days

Document any days your child is sick. If there is any discrepancy between your dates and what the school notes, you have documentation.

Behavior

Everyone has an "off" day now and then, but if you notice your child is unusually tired after school, or if he or she has a change in eating habits, make a quick note on the date. This will help you be able to quickly identify patterns or anomalies in your child's behavior.

"No Homework" Days

When your child states that they do not have homework, make a quick note on the calendar. If you see a trend, it may be time to send that teacher a quick message to investigate.

Over time making these quick notes daily will provide you with an abundance of information to help you keep up with your child's school life. When you go to the parent-teacher conference and take your binder, it will show the teacher that you are serious about your child's education.

TEACHER CONTACT INFORMATION

Create one page that lists teacher contact information for all children; include the teachers' email addresses for easy and direct contact.

CASH POUCH

Keep a pouch with cash for those times your child informs you that they need money for a school activity or lunch as they head out the door in the morning.

INDIVIDUAL FOLDERS

Include a folder for each child. Keep activity schedules on one side of the folder; the second side is for any forms you need to sign and send back to school. Behind each child's folder, place four sheet protectors or plastic pockets. The first pocket stores report cards for the current year. The second pocket can store medical or physical forms that need to be kept for various activities. The third pocket holds information that pertains to various activities (that clarinet rental agreement!). Finally, the fourth pocket is used to keep miscellaneous items, such as school fundraiser information.

BACK-TO-SCHOOL INFORMATION

You may want to include a section in your binder for information such as school supply shopping lists, registration paperwork, and other helpful back-to-school forms.

A parent binder will save valuable time and keep the front of your fridge from becoming a cluttered bulletin board! If you are a parent who travels a lot, or if you prefer using technology instead of a physical binder, you can easily incorporate the same system using an online calendar.

CHAPTER SEVEN

BEDROOMS
The Rejuvenation Spaces

One thing that brings me great joy when working with clients is the contrast in the tone of our conversations from the beginning of the process to the end. I worked with a client who was extremely frustrated by the guest bedroom in her home. The room was also used as an office and an exercise room. There were piles of paperwork on the floor and the various pieces of exercise equipment felt awkward in the space.

This particular client had a very busy life: she worked full-time running her own business. For years she had children at home, and her elderly parents also lived with her. During this time, my client's home was understandably low on her list of priorities. However, as her lifestyle changed—her children grew up and moved out and her parents were no longer living with her—my client found herself surrounded by clutter and overwhelmed by the disorganization in her home.

When we began our first session, my client felt a sense of urgency about her guest bedroom because she was expecting a guest the very next weekend. However, I still took the time to talk at length with my client to better understand her lifestyle. Now that she and her husband were empty nesters, they suddenly had three empty, unused bedrooms—but they were still living as though they had six people living in the house full-time. By the end of our first session together, my client had gone from being frustrated and overwhelmed to optimistic and excited. We realized that we could transform one of the spare bedrooms into an exercise room and another into a home office, leaving the third spare room to be used solely as a guest bedroom. My client had found new reasons to fall in love with her home!

After a long day of work, school, running errands, and meeting life's many obligations, we all need somewhere peaceful to retreat, a space for respite from our busy lives. The bedroom should be a space to rejuvenate so that you can feel refreshed and prepared to take on the world again the next day. This is why it is so important for this space to be well-organized, beautiful, and serene, free from clutter and distractions.

STEP ONE: ASSESS YOUR SPACE

Bedrooms are personal retreats and their primary purpose is to promote rest and relaxation. As such, it is essential to keep the organization straightforward and décor simple but elegant. Include only furniture pieces that are strictly necessary. In our bedroom, I prefer to store all of our clothing in the closet, so I eschew an armoire and dresser. It is simply more practical for me to keep my clothing in one central location. Even better, this creates space in the bedroom to incorporate a settee or chaise lounge chair. As you consider your bedroom, think about what items truly bring you comfort. Streamline your wardrobe to fit the space you have and organize other items efficiently. Begin to think of your bedroom as your retreat, rather than as a place to store things. Think of how you might make it feel like a luxurious boutique hotel, a space to encourage rest, relaxation, and rejuvenation.

STEP TWO: *DECLUTTER* YOUR SPACE

The bedroom is a space that can easily accumulate clutter if you do not make a concerted effort to keep the space tidy and serene. Before you begin to clean and organize, first thoroughly declutter your bedroom. Here are a few tips and tricks to help you navigate through typically tricky clutter pitfalls:

◁ GENERAL CLUTTER ▷

I discourage my clients from including items in their bedrooms that involve any sort of work, such as desks, filing cabinets, or exercise equipment. Here's a simple rule of thumb: any item that does not serve to either help you get ready for the day or relax you should be relocated to elsewhere in your home.

◁ CLOSET CLUTTER ▷

Closets are often major clutter zones! Methodically work your way through your clothing and shoes. If something doesn't fit or is damaged, or if you simply haven't worn that item in years, relieve yourself of it. It is only taking up space and adding both physical and mental clutter.

◁ JEWELRY CLUTTER ▷

Oftentimes, the jewelry we own is strictly sentimental. Perhaps you inherited or were gifted certain pieces from family members. Maybe it's that 1989 class ring that you feel you shouldn't part with. I do tend to make exceptions with jewelry as pieces can often be passed down through generations, but I still encourage you to be highly selective with the items that you hold onto. Sometimes, heirloom items may hold monetary value. Whether the value of a piece is tied to sentiment or money, think about storing these items appropriately in a safety deposit box or in a secure, fireproof home safe.

Just as with clothing, you should occasionally declutter your jewelry collection. There are a few things to consider as you do so:

Fashion Jewelry

Do you have items that are missing a bead or a clasp? Are these items in otherwise excellent condition and worth repair? Sometimes, fashion jewelry can become worn and no longer wearable; these items should be purged. If most of your items are in excellent condition, consider each piece and ask if it fits your current style. If the answer is "no," then it is time to donate those pieces. A great option is to research local organizations to see if they accept jewelry donation. I admire Dress for Success®, a non-profit organization that empowers women to achieve economic independence.

Fine Jewelry

Because fine jewelry is more valuable, it can feel even more difficult to purge items from your collection. Add a sentimental factor, and that the difficulty level increases. If you have beautiful jewelry that you do not wear, a good first step is to have it appraised. It's essential to establish the value of any piece before you attempt to sell it. If a piece of jewelry is sentimental but not a piece that you would wear, you might consider having it altered into something that is more to your taste.

STEP THREE: CLEAN YOUR SPACE

Keeping your bedroom free of dust can actually improve the quality of your sleep. Dust doesn't collect only on the surface of furniture, however. As you clean your bedroom, be sure to vacuum underneath your bed and behind furniture. Wipe down baseboard and window sills.

Change your bedding at least once a week. It can be helpful to have at least one spare set of sheets; this will allow you to put clean sheets on your bed as soon as you remove the soiled sheets.

When you remove your clothing, do not simply leave it piled on the floor or draped across a piece of furniture. Instead, hang up items that don't need to be laundered right away. Soiled items should be placed directly into a laundry basket or bag.

Above all, commit to staying on top of clutter. Once you have deep-cleaned your bedroom, take a few minutes each day to tidy up your bedroom! Dust and vacuum weekly and do a deep clean of your bedroom at least once a season.

STEP FOUR: ORGANIZE YOUR SPACE

◁ BED ORGANIZATION ▷

The bed is the centerpiece of the bedroom. Of course, it's important to have a comfortable space to lay your head at night, but also consider the potential the bed has for organizing purposes. After all, the bed is the piece of furniture that takes up the majority of space in a bedroom, so it makes sense to make the most of that space.

Under-bed Storage

Utilize the space under the bed for storage. I like to store bed linens under the beds in each room. This makes it simple and convenient when it comes time to change the bedding. There are a variety of under-bed storage options that will keep items neatly stored and protected. This is an especially helpful solution for those living in small spaces.

TIP

Bed linens can be difficult to fold neatly. One way to attractively store your linens is to purchase plain, inexpensive pillowcases and have them embroidered with the sheet sizes. When you pull sheets out of the dryer, simply roll them and place them in the appropriate pillowcase. No one will ever know that your sheets are not folded to perfection!

Bed Caddy

A bed caddy is a small organizer that tucks into the side of a mattress, making it simple to access items from bed. You can easily store magazines, water, or the remote control, freeing your nightstand from items that may make it feel cluttered. Bed caddies can even be concealed by bedding.

◁ *NIGHTSTAND ORGANIZATION* ▷

Many people struggle to keep their bedside table organized. To organize your nightstand, think of items in three main categories: comfort, safety, and prep.

Comfort

READING MATERIAL I keep my Bible at my bedside; reading it is the way that both I start and end my day, and this gives me a sense of personal comfort. For me, it is a bedside must-have.

BASICS Some comfort basics include tissues, hand cream, lip balm, an eye mask, and water.

LUXURY Luxury items contribute to the experience of your bedroom as a retreat; items such as face mist, essential oils, or moisture socks can make you feel special and pampered.

Safety

MOBILE PHONE I used to believe that it was disruptive to my rest to have my cell phone near my bedside. I still believe this to be true, but after experiencing an emergency situation that required me to call 911 quickly, I feel more secure with it near me when I sleep. It is important to turn notifications off; I opt to leave my ringer on in case a family emergency occurs during the night. I also remember to charge my phone before going to bed.

FLASHLIGHT It is smart and helpful to keep a flashlight near the bedside for middle-of-the-night power outages.

EYEGLASSES If you wear contacts or glasses, keep a pair of glasses nearby in case you need to get up in the middle of the night.

MEDICATION If you use any medications you might urgently need during the night, it's a good idea to keep these near your bed. However, if you have small children or pets in your home, be sure to secure your medication. Medicine lock boxes are sold online specifically for this purpose.

Prep

ALARM CLOCK If you need to wake up at a particular time (as most of us do), a stylish alarm clock can give you a great start to your morning.

NOTEPAD AND PEN Often while in bed, I think of something I need to remember, or I occasionally come up with a brilliant idea. With a notepad and pen nearby, I can quickly jot a note to follow-up on so the thought doesn't nag me all night.

◁ CLOSET ORGANIZATION ▷

As I noted earlier in this chapter, closets can easily become overrun by unworn, ill-fitting, or tired clothing. Once you have thoroughly decluttered, here are some tips to keep your closet and the items in it neatly and attractively displayed:

Clothing and Shoes

To create a barrier for clutter, identify a reasonable number of hangers for each item: pants, skirts, suits, dresses, shirts, and so on. This gives you a guide to how many things to allow in your closet space at any given time. For example, if you know that you wear seven pairs of pants in a week's time, then you might allow yourself a limit of fourteen hangers for pants.

Apply the same concept to shoes. I like to use shoe boxes to store each pair of my shoes. I label the boxes so that I can easily see all the pairs of shoes that I own. I allow myself a certain number of boxes; I won't allow myself to purchase more pairs of shoes than I have boxes for. If my boxes are full and I do buy a new pair of shoes, I know that I will need to give away an old pair to make way for the new. This strategy will help you to prevent overindulging and limits your closet to contain only items that you truly wear.

Handbags and Accessories

I love a beautiful handbag and other fun accessories, but they can become unmanageable if I don't set limitations and stick to an organized system. I like to use my handbags as the "decor" of my closet. They are already beautiful, so they are a perfect accessory with which to decorate my closet.

I prefer to organize my accessories by category. For example, I keep wallets, coin purses, and other accessories that go inside handbags sorted by color in little baskets; this allows me to quickly find the right pieces to coordinate with whatever handbag I am using. Alternately, you can actually store coordinating pieces inside the purse they go with, making it easy to grab the bag you want and go. I do strongly recommend that when you switch bags, you take the time to completely clean out the bag you are finished using; it will be ready the next time you want to use it, and it's also the best way to keep your handbags in good condition.

◁ JEWELRY ORGANIZATION ▷

My favorite jewelry organizers are trays. They are beautiful and versatile, allowing you to organize your jewelry so that it is visible and accessible. Smaller trays can be used to pre-plan jewelry for the day or week ahead, which can save you time getting ready each day.

I also love to see jewelry displayed in a closet area. This is a great opportunity to showcase colorful pieces, making your closet feel a bit like a boutique. There are many decorative wall pieces that offer a beautiful way to organize and display favorite jewelry pieces. If you live in a small space, a jewelry hanger is a great option for storing jewelry. Since it hangs in the closet with your clothes, a jewelry hanger can also be discreetly hidden.

STEP FIVE: *BEAUTIFY* YOUR SPACE

Bedroom décor should enhance the feeling of peace and relaxation you are striving for. Choose bedding in colors you find soothing; select artwork that conveys the look or feel that you appreciate in your rejuvenation space.

You may wish to infuse scent in your bedroom space, either through diffusers or subtly scented candles. Select scent with care: lavender, for example, can help to promote a feeling of relaxation to ease you to sleep each evening.

If you are easily disturbed by noises in the night, the white noise of a sound machine may help you to rest easy.

Likewise, if you are easily woken by light in the morning, consider installing blackout shades or curtains in your bedroom. Also keep other sources of light—even from your alarm clock—to a minimum. Studies show that any source of light during the night can have a detrimental effect on the quality of your sleep.

Keep your décor simple and focused on quality, with a feeling of luxury and elegance for sound sleep and sweet dreams.

CREATE AN EXPERIENCE:
THE BED OF YOUR DREAMS

The bed is the central, essential piece of furniture in the bedroom, the place where you spend so much of your time, so it makes sense to put effort toward making your bed comfortable—even luxuriously so. The bed is also generally the focal point of the bedroom. For both aesthetic and practical reasons, investing in your bed and bedding is well worth it.

◁ MATTRESS ▷

Do you get enough hours of sleep but still wake up feeling tired? Your mattress may be partially to blame. A bad mattress can leave you feeling sore and unrested. It is essential to have a quality mattress. A mattress is a considerable financial investment, so take care in making your purchase. Don't be afraid to test out mattresses in the store before you make your purchase. Many stores will allow a "trial period" so you can test the mattress in your home.

To properly maintain your mattress and ensure that it wears evenly, rotate the mattress 180 degrees every six months. Pillow-top mattresses do not need to be flipped over; mattresses without a pillow-top can be flipped every six months.

Whether you have an existing mattress or are purchasing a new mattress, there are luxury items that can add an additional level of comfort:

Mattress Topper

A mattress topper adds a layer of comfort to your bed, but choose your topper with care. For example, if you tend to get hot at night, you may want to avoid latex or memory foam toppers that retain body heat. If you love a soft surface, you may enjoy a feather mattress topper. Some toppers even offer infused aromatherapy to help relax you.

TIP

For added luxury, layer a down topper on a 3-inch memory foam pad.

Mattress Cover

Some people are very sensitive to dust and other allergens. A washable mattress cover can help to keep allergens at bay. I am a huge believer that every bed should have a

waterproof mattress cover to protect your mattress from moisture, dust mites, and odor. This is especially important in children's bedrooms and guest bedrooms. Think of a mattress cover as a way to protect the investment you have made in a quality mattress!

◁ BED PILLOWS ▷

Do not underestimate the importance of proper pillows. Your pillow impacts how your body and spine align when you are in bed. Proper alignment helps to prevent neck and back pain.

BASIC PILLOW GUIDE

PILLOW TYPE	PROS	CONS
Memory Foam Pillows	Great support; won't get lumpy	Very firm; can be hot
Down Pillows	Plush and cozy	More expensive; requires fluffing; more difficult to clean
Feather Pillows	Soft; will conform to your body	Will flatten easily and may not be as cooling
Down Alternative Pillows	Soft and cooling	Less durable; can get lumpy
Synthetic Fill Pillows	Easy-to-wash so ideal for allergy sufferers	Can easily attract dust mites; no ventilation; short life span
Buckwheat Pillow	Supportive and cooling	Noisy and heavy
Latex Pillow	Great support and cooling; mold and mildew resistant (great for damp climates)	Not good for anyone with latex allergies; heavy and not breathable
Microbead Pillows	Cooling and moldable	Can be messy if microbeads fall out; noisy; may not fit all standard pillow cases
Water Pillow	Supportive and pain relieving	Risk of leaks; very firm
Cotton Pillow	Cooling and allergy-free; washable	Flattens and clumps over time; needs to be cleaned often to prevent dust mites and mold
Wool Pillow	Breathable and allergy-free	Can easily flatten; dry clean only
Gel Pillow	Cooling; great complement with other pillows such as memory foam pillows	Not as cozy or soft as other pillow options
Bamboo Pillows	Conforms to body; will adapt to all temperatures	Must stay dry; heavy pillow

I recommend incorporating multiple pillows: two pillows for a twin bed, and four pillows for a queen or king-sized bed. Consider providing two types of pillows on each bed for comfort and choice. If you select down or feather pillows, be sure to select from a company that guarantees their feathers are harvested in a cruelty-free manner.

◁ BED LINENS ▷

While many of us are reluctant to spend one hundred and fifty dollars on a set of luxury sheets that will bring years of comfort, we may easily spend that much a month on our coffee runs! Given the number of hours that we spend wrapped in our bed linens, I am a big believer in investing in quality luxury linens. After all, these are items that impact the quality of our rest. A good night's sleep has a huge benefit; anything that may help you rest well is a worthy investment.

TIP

Always carefully read labels before you make a purchase. Did you know that manufacturers often put a silicon coating on their bedsheets to make them smooth to the touch? Only after a few washes does the true quality (or lack thereof) of the sheets become evident.

Shopping for quality bed linens is a straightforward process. Consider three key factors:

Color

White, white, and more white! White sheets are the way to go to bring a luxurious feel to your bedding. Slipping into a bed of white sheets is like a breath of fresh air, and after a long day that is just what most of us need. I also love the fact that white sheets are so versatile. They can be easily coordinated with other fabrics and textures.

Fabric

Percale, sateen, or linen? We all have different preferences for the texture and feel of our bedsheets. Decide what feel you prefer before you invest in quality linens.

Bedding Layers

The climate where you live, the season of the year, and your own personal tendencies to feel either very hot or very cold at night all influence the number and type of blankets, quilts, or comforters you may wish to include on your bed. In colder climates or in winter months, you may layer a number of blankets; in the summer, a simple top sheet and quilt may suffice. Your preferences for texture and colors should also come into play.

Remember: in choosing your bedding, you are creating the zone of ultimate comfort in your home. It is well worth the investment—both in time and money!

THE GUEST BEDROOM

The guest bedroom is one of the simplest places to maintain in my home. I am always sure to clean and organize the space right after a guest departs; this means that I do not have to do anything aside from routine dusting and vacuuming until we have another overnight guest.

I love the art of making my guest feel special and welcome, and our guest bedroom allows me the opportunity to treat guests like royalty. It's important to me that our guests have a lovely experience in our home; I believe that a guest bedroom is a special place to create a beautiful experience, almost like a boutique hotel.

◁ CREATING A DUAL SPACE ▷

It can be difficult to carve out space to use solely as a guest room. If you are working with limited space in your home, a great way to get everyday use out of your guest space is to set it up as a multi-use room. A guest room can double as an office or craft room. When you have guests, the space can be converted to a guest bedroom. If you do opt for a multi-use guest room, however, it becomes even more important to create organization systems to keep the room tidy and functional. For example, you will need to decide if you want to have a standard bed in the space, or if you would rather have a convertible sofa, a Murphy bed, or even a portable option like a rollaway bed that you pull out only when you have guests. There is no wrong or right choice; you have a wide variety of options to choose what works best for your home and your guests.

◁ GUEST BEDROOM PREPARATION ▷

Designate a space for your guest room. As a first step in organizing the space, declutter and clean as described in chapter one. It can be easy to let this space become a collection zone all for other things in your home, which makes it feel like a storage unit rather than a beautiful, dedicated space for your guests. Whether the space functions solely as a guest bedroom or a dual-purpose space, it is important to establish guidelines for you and your family to keep this area in order.

◁ GUEST BEDROOM BEDDING ▷

There are a few essential items to incorporate into your guest space. Remember, this is a space that will accommodate multiple people; as such, I treat the guest room differently than other areas in my home.

Mattress and Pillow Covers

I recommend using a mattress cover on the guest room bed and pillow covers on the pillows. Since you likely host a variety of guests, this will allow you to keep things sanitary. If you are likely to have young guests, you might even consider a waterproof mattress pad.

Duvet

I suggest using a duvet on your guest bed instead of a comforter. A duvet is easier to remove and wash after a guest visit. Duvets are easy to fold and store; you can keep spare duvets on hand and change out linens for the different seasons.

◁ GUEST BEDROOM CLOSET ▷

I believe that a gracious host considers the comfort of her guests. It's thoughtful to provide a clear space where guests can unpack their clothes and store their luggage. Ideally, you should keep guest room closet space as open as possible. Keep a supply of spare hangers in the closet. I also like to keep a set of spare linens available so that guests can change the bedding if necessary. Keep the closet organization simple, with items clearly visible. I use unlined, labeled baskets so that my guests can easily identify items they need. If you use your guest room closet for household storage, you might instead place a dresser or a luggage rack in the room for your guests to use.

GUEST BEDROOM IN A BAG

It can be challenging to make an overnight guest feel comfortable when you live in a small space and lack a dedicated guest bedroom. I have been in this situation several times, so I came up with the "Guest Bedroom in a Bag." This is a way for you to always feel prepared to make your guests feel special. You can easily store this bag under your own bed for convenience. Even if you are lucky and have a guest bedroom, you may still have times when you do not have enough bedrooms to accommodate the number of guests you have visiting. The "Guest Bedroom in a Bag" can save the day!

What *is* a "Guest Bedroom in a Bag"? It is simply a bag that contains all of the essentials to make your guests feel comfortable.

◁ BATHROBE ▷

A luxurious bathrobe will make a guest feel pampered and comfy. I prefer to offer a classic white robe because it allows guests to see that the robe is fresh and clean. Many bathrobes are one size fits all and can accommodate guests of all sizes.

◁ BEVERAGE ▷

I like to keep a both a nice bottle of wine and bottled water on hand for guests. These items can be stored in the guest bag so that you have them in the event of last-minute surprise guests. However, refrain from adding food items to the bag!

◁ TOWELS ▷

Guests appreciate fresh, fluffy towels. Be sure to include enough bath towels, hand towels, and washcloths for several guests.

◁ SHEETS ▷

I keep an extra set of sheets in my "Guest Bedroom in a Bag." I like to place the sheets in a beautifully monogrammed pillowcase.

◁ LIGHTING ▷

If your guests will sleep on an air mattress, it's a nice touch to include a mini light in the bag in case they want to read at night or a little light when they sleep. Choose a light that folds down and is easy to store.

◁ SOMETHING SPECIAL ▷

I love to include a few small touches to make my guests feel truly welcome. You could pre-write a welcome note on pretty stationery, select a novel by a local author, or even include a locally-published magazine. Often, these magazines can be found for free at your local grocery store.

◁ WI-FI ACCESS CODE ▷

Make it simple for your guests to access Wi-Fi; create a cute card with your home wi-fi code. I always appreciate when someone makes this information readily available to me when I am the visitor.

CHAPTER EIGHT

BATHROOM
The Cleansing Space

O ne of the joys of being a professional organizer is being able to show my clients that they have more than enough space in their homes. With creative thinking and the proper systems in place, even a shoebox apartment can be beautifully organized! I once worked with a client who insisted that her bathroom didn't offer adequate storage for her items.

Before my initial tour of this client's home, I anticipated that she would have an excess of products. This is true for approximately 95 percent of the people I work with, and it was certainly true for this client, too! However, I reserved judgment and began to ask questions, with a goal to understand her usual routines in this space. This information helped me to realize what she truly needed in the bathroom area so that we could eliminate unnecessary clutter.

I discovered that my client had a weekly hair maintenance process. She also had an intense dental hygiene routine that involved far more than just a toothbrush and dental floss. In addition, she had a multi-step daily facial care routine that included a variety of products. Last, it was evident that my client had a hobby of collecting hotel toiletries!

We determined that we could streamline my client's various personal care routines—and therefore streamline her bathroom organization—by separating her many products into categories by their purpose. She used beautiful, large zippered makeup bags to sort her products: facial care products went in one bag, dental hygiene products in another, and so on. The zippered bags served to categorize items by their use, and they also effectively set a space limit to prevent my client from overindulging in excess products. We also gathered the luxury hotel toiletries she had amassed into a single container and relocated these items to the guest bedroom.

◇

The bathroom is a space in which streamlined and efficient organization is essential. It is a room that is typically shared by multiple people, and a place where a variety of products are used and stored. In other words, the bathroom is an organization disaster waiting to happen! It doesn't have to be this way, though. With careful attention to the people, products, and organization solutions, your bathroom space can be a beautiful and serene area in your home.

STEP ONE: *ASSESS* YOUR BATHROOM

As you consider your bathroom, first think about who the primary users of the space are. Are you attempting to organize your master bathroom? A hallway bathroom shared by teenagers? Or perhaps you would like to dedicate a bathroom space for guest use. Each person who uses the bathroom will need space to store their own personal care items. Because most bathrooms are shared by multiple people, each family member should abide by the same expectations for keeping the space tidy—no towels on the bathroom floor or uncapped toothpaste next to the sink! Hint: this may be a good topic for a Family Home Meeting (see pages 22–23).

STEP TWO: *DECLUTTER* YOUR BATHROOM

Keeping in mind the needs of the people who utilize the bathroom, begin the decluttering process. The bathroom is home to personal hygiene products. These products are consumable; as such, when the product has been used up, the container should be discarded. That seems pretty straightforward, right? On the contrary: in my experience as a professional organizer, I meet many people who are product hoarders. The trouble begins when they buy a new product and don't like it, don't use it, or both. These excess products can quickly lead to an accumulation of clutter.

It's time for that critical word again: *limitations*. Set limits for yourself to avoid hoarding products. As with every other space, clutter causes frustration and leaves you feeling overwhelmed. I have found that having designated areas for specific items allows me to keep the perfect amount of product on hand in my bathroom space. For example, in our linen closet, my husband and I each have one bin allotted for our bath products. We also each keep a separate tray for luxury products.

Here are some other ways to eliminate clutter and streamline the items in your bathroom:

◁ DISCARD PACKAGING ▷

Remove items from their store packaging and house them in storage bins whenever possible. This makes efficient use of your space and it is easy to access an item when you need it.

◁ TAKE INVENTORY ▷

Determine the appropriate number of bath towels, hand towels, and washcloths for each family member for each week (or however often you wash laundry). This helps you to limit your linen closet to the items you need. When towels and linens become worn, it is time to purge and replace.

TIP

One of my friends recently shared that she donates used towels to a local animal shelter, giving the towels a second life.

◁ *PURGE EXPIRED COSMETICS* ▷

Although I do wear makeup, my cosmetic collection is minimal. With all of the makeup gurus on the internet and the many advertisements that encourage us to try new products, it's easy to end up with a cluttered makeup bag. When I help clients to declutter their homes, I frequently notice expired makeup. It's important to know that makeup and most other personal products have a shelf life. Since we apply makeup to our bodies and because cosmetic products can hold bacteria, it is imperative to be mindful of expiration dates on cosmetics and to purge products in a timely manner.

There are no laws in the United States that require cosmetic companies to put expiration dates on their products, but you will find that some manufacturers place a PAO (Period-After-Opening) symbol on their product. This lets you know how many months the product is suitable for use after it has been opened. For cosmetics lacking a PAO symbol, I use this general guide when purging makeup:

MAKEUP SPONGE: 1 month
MASCARA: 4 to 6 months
LIQUID EYELINER: 4 to 6 months
BLUSH: 18 months
BRONZER: 18 months
EYESHADOW: 18 months
EYELINER: 18 months

CONCEALER: 1 year
FOUNDATION: 1 year
MOISTURIZER: 1 year
NAIL POLISH: 1 to 2 years
LIPLINER: 1 year
LIPSTICK: 18 months to two years
LIP GLOSS: 18 months to two years

NOTE: If your makeup starts to have a foul odor, becomes clumpy, or changes color, it is likely expired.

STEP THREE: *CLEAN YOUR BATHROOM*

I must admit that cleaning the bathroom is my least favorite thing to do. This is why it is especially crucial for me to have a simple and efficient method to keep things clean in this space. Because most bathrooms get a lot of activity, a consistent routine is essential.

◁ DEEP CLEANING ▷

Once you have decluttered your bathroom, the next step is to give your bathroom a thorough cleaning. Wipe down shelves and inside cabinets; thoroughly scrub the shower, sink, and toilet. This is also a good time to wipe down doors, baseboards, walls, and to mop the floor. (Don't be afraid to wash the floor on your hands and knees for extra shine!)

Of course, a clean bathroom won't stay clean for long. I find it useful to follow daily, weekly, and monthly cleaning routines for the bathrooms in my home.

◁ DAILY REFRESH ▷

The easiest way to create a simple daily routine is to follow your everyday habits in the space and add a cleaning component for each part of your routine. For example, keep a shower spray near the shower. As you get out of the shower, give it a few sprays. No scrubbing required!

Keep a pack of cleaning wipes near your makeup bag. After you remove your makeup each night, use a cleaning wipe to give the sink a quick clean. Keep a small, handheld vacuum under your sink or in your bathroom linen closet to easily remove hair and dust. I find it useful to give the toilet a quick clean after the last use of the day. Finally, at the end of the day, use a disinfectant wipe to hit those bathroom germ hot spots such as the light switch, faucets, door handles, and toilet handle. These simple habits can reduce the time needed for your weekly cleaning.

◁ WEEKLY SPARKLE ▷

When you have a daily refresh routine in place, it allows you to focus your weekly cleaning to give your bathroom a beautiful sparkle.

I find it helpful to create steps to clean the bathroom, just as I have steps to wash my face. I follow a clean, tone, and moisturize routine for my face, and I follow a clean, disinfect, and shine routine while cleaning my bathroom. Create a cleaning caddy to aid with this three-step process. (You can even label your cleaning bottles with "Clean," "Disinfect," and "Shine.")

You can also set a timer for the amount of time you want to allow yourself to clean your bathroom; this can keep you focused and motivated and helps you to follow your bathroom cleaning routine. A timer will demonstrate that it does not take as long as you think to clean your bathroom, even though dread of the task can make it feel daunting!

◁ MONTHLY MAINTENANCE ▷

Even with daily and weekly cleaning, it's necessary to dedicate time each month to address deeper cleaning and organization needs in your bathroom. Repeat these tasks at least monthly to keep your bathroom functioning to perfection:

Stock Up

Use a notepad and take inventory of your bathroom to ensure that you have everything you need for the upcoming month: soap, toothpaste, toilet paper, cleaning products, etc. A good rule is to have a month's supply of each item. This will keep you from product hoarding, but also prevent you from feeling like you need to run to the store each week.

Tidy Linen Closet

Get into that linen closet and give it a quick primping. If towels are disheveled, straighten them. If items are out of place or things need to be removed, this is the time. You can also sneak a beautiful luxury bar of soap in the back of the cabinet so that you are welcomed with a lovely scent when you open the closet door.

Make-up Drawer or Bag Clean Out

Once a month, go through your makeup bag or drawer and discard any old make-up. Take inventory of any products you need to replace. Give the area a quick cleaning.

Under Sink

Pull the items from under the sink and wipe down the inside and outside of the cabinet. This gives you the opportunity to organize the items neatly as you put them back into place.

Floors, Doors, Baseboards, and Walls

At least once a month, give these areas a thorough clean. Use hot, soapy water and a microfiber cloth and wipe down your baseboards and walls. This is also the time to thoroughly mop the bathroom floor (although you'll want to mop weekly, too). Add a few drops of your favorite essential oil for a fresh scent in the bathroom.

STEP FOUR: ORGANIZE YOUR BATHROOM

Like the kitchen, the bathroom typically has a number of distinct areas, each with its own organizational needs. Begin the process of organizing your bathroom by establishing a system to effectively manage the variety of products typically utilized in this space. Each category of products should have their own "home," whether housed in the shower, under the sink, or in a linen closet.

◁ COSMETICS AND PERSONAL PRODUCTS ▷

The client whose story you read at the beginning of this chapter used a wide variety of products. If you recall, we were able to establish an effective "category" system that helped her to keep products organized and accessible. Consider applying the same concept in your own bathroom.

Create an Everyday Cosmetics Kit

Most of us have an everyday makeup routine that involves only certain cosmetic items. I like to keep a small makeup caddy that holds my everyday makeup essentials. This simplifies my morning routine, saving me valuable time on busy mornings because I don't need to rummage to locate my daily essentials. It also makes traveling simple because I'm always prepared. Use a miniature makeup case or small makeup bag and tuck it away near the area where you typically apply your makeup.

◁ SHOWER ORGANIZATION ▷

Many bathrooms have a bathtub-shower combination. The shower can feel cramped; however, a curved shower curtain rod can make the shower feel more expansive, providing extra elbow room in the shower's interior. Even with ample elbow-room, however, the shower is best organized by minimizing the number of products in the space. You may even consider installing a mounted dispenser in your shower to keep it clutter-free.

◁ UNDER-SINK ORGANIZATION ▷

A bathroom with under-sink storage offers a great space to store frequently-used items. However, it is important

to incorporate ways to keep this space tidy and organized. Baskets or bins can help to corral products. There are many shelves, drawers, and other organizational tools made specifically for under-sink organization!

◁ LINEN CLOSET ORGANIZATION ▷

It is easier than you might expect to maintain an organized linen closet. As with any space you are organizing, it's best to start with a blank canvas. Remove all items from your linen closet. As you consider the now-empty space, allow your mind to think creatively about how to arrange the space in a way that works for well you and your family. Have a plan for how you want to arrange your linen closet before you begin to return items to the shelves.

When you have an idea of how you want the space to be organized, think about how you can enhance the experience you have when you when you open the linen closet. I love to open my linen closet and breathe in the fresh scent as I enjoy the sight of expertly folded towels and rows of luxury products. This simple experience brings me joy. Once you envision your ideal experience in your mind, it is time to make your vision a reality.

Incorporate Storage

Linen closets often store much more than bed sheets and bath towels! Bath products, toilet paper, and other personal hygiene products can be housed in a linen closet. Keep like items in your linen closet grouped together and discreetly concealed in attractive storage bins or baskets; these make the space visually appealing by cutting down on the number of visible items in the closet, and they also help your family members recognize where items belong and prevent the closet from becoming overstuffed.

Commit to a Color

The linen closet is yet another space where it can be beneficial to assign a different color to each family member, a visual cue that creates accountability for keeping items tidy by returning them to their appropriate places. (Color-coded towels are particularly useful; you will quickly notice missing towels, making it difficult for family members to hoard dirty towels in their bedrooms!)

STEP FIVE: *BEAUTIFY* YOUR BATHROOM

A bathroom is functional, and there is no reason it cannot also be beautiful. After all, this is where you get ready for the day each morning, and where you get ready for bed each evening. Shouldn't the bathroom be pleasant and inviting?

For inspiration, I always think of my favorite day spa as well as luxury hotels that I have stayed in.

◁ *TOWELS* ▷

Don't skimp on towels! It is worth it to spend a bit more on thick, luxurious, absorbent towels and washcloths. These are a pleasure to use each day, and they actually last longer than their cheap counterparts!

◁ *SCENT* ▷

In addition to a freshly scented linen closet, you may enjoy keeping a scented candle or diffuser on your bathroom vanity. Select bath products in your favorite scent; the aroma you love for your skin and hair will also linger in your bathroom throughout the day.

◁ LUXURY ITEMS ▷

Purchase an attractive glass or ceramic soap dispenser in lieu of plastic soap dispensers. Not only are these beautiful, but they are also environmentally-friendly! Treat yourself to your favorite luxury bath products; these make daily routines a pleasure. If you have wall space, display interesting artwork. Floor rugs and shower curtains can be inexpensive ways to add a high-end look to your bathroom.

CREATE AN EXPERIENCE:
THE POWDER ROOM & GUEST BATHROOM

Because powder rooms and guest bathrooms are intended for guests, it is essential that these spaces are spotless, simplified, and user-friendly. I want my guests to have the sense that the space is for them, and not that they have just entered my personal bathroom. With proper organization, powder rooms and guest bathrooms can be beautiful and take minimal effort to maintain.

Keep only necessary items in the powder room and guest bathroom. Make it simple for guests to find what they need; do not store anything beyond what is useful. However, items for these spaces should feel luxurious and welcoming to send a message to your guests that they are important to you. It may be just a bathroom, but I love to arrange every space in my home in a manner that creates an enjoyable experience. Consider these essentials as you refresh and organize the powder room and guest bathroom:

◁ HAND SOAP ▷

An essential item in a powder room and guest bathroom, hand soap can be beautifully presented in a variety of ways:

Liquid Hand Soap

Liquid hand soap is commonly found in bathrooms; it is easy to replace and user-friendly. I recommend that you supply hypoallergenic hand soap for guests, especially if you are transferring it into an unlabeled dispenser. I prefer simple, elegant clear glass dispensers, making it easy to see when the soap needs to be replenished. For beautiful presentation, insert a piece of rosemary into the bottle before you fill it with soap.

Bar Soap

Bar soap is a beautiful option for the guest bathroom or powder room, though it is more difficult to maintain a spotless space as you will need to frequently clean the soap tray. Bar soap may also harbor germs, which would certainly be unpleasant for a guest. However, you might consider placing a beautiful bowl filled with soap leaves or soap flower petals next to the sink. This is beautiful and enhances the bathroom space for your guest; it is also practical as each lovely leaf or petal is intended for a single use.

Powder Soap

Powder soap offers a spa-like experience for your guest. A number of brands sell high-end, beautiful dry powdered hand soap. This soap looks gorgeous placed in a beautiful wooden bowl with a small scoop.

◁ TOILET PAPER ▷

While there is nothing particularly glamorous about toilet paper, it is still an item that should be displayed with care. You can do this with a bit of style (and yes, it is bizarre to use the words "style" and "toilet paper" together!). Think about folding back the corners of the toilet paper to create a triangle, just as they do in luxury hotels. (I am an avid observer of the elegant touches in high-end hotels, as they have invested a lot into providing guests with a five-star experience. These tips and tricks that I pick up serve as excellent sources of inspiration for my own home!)

I like to put a few drops of essential oil on the inner cardboard toilet paper roll before I place it on the dispenser. A subtle, pleasant fragrance is released when the roll turns.

TIP

Powder rooms often lack under-sink cabinet storage. To ensure you have enough toilet paper on hand for guests, consider installing a double toilet paper holder that stores two rolls instead of just a single role, or incorporate a free-standing toilet paper holder with storage.

◁ *HAND TOWELS* ▷

I have a love-hate relationship with hand towels in the powder room. It's obviously necessary to have a way to dry one's hands, and hand towels are also often beautiful and a fun way to decorate the bathroom. However, I dislike having only one hand towel in such a high-traffic area. It doesn't seem sanitary. When I go to someone's home, I always wonder if the hand towel is clean. In my own home, I opt to offer inexpensive washcloths in lieu of a single hand towel. This practice was inspired by my favorite spa. When I visit the spa for a manicure, I love the pristine white washcloths, an upgrade from a rough paper towel that adds a special touch to my visit. To recreate this experience in my home bathroom, I buy inexpensive bundles of white washcloths. I roll each washcloth and I even tuck a mini, single-use lotion pod in the center as a pleasant surprise. To save space, I place the washcloths on a shelf hanging on the powder room wall. You could also display the rolled washcloths on a decorative tray if you have adequate countertop space. It's useful to have a basket or wall-mounted towel hanger in the bathroom for guests to place used washcloths.

◁ *TOILETRIES FOR GUESTS* ▷

In my guest bathroom, I create a one-stop shop in the under-sink cabinet with everything my guests may need or want on hand. To organize the cabinet, I line like items together on beautiful, rectangular porcelain trays. I select products from the same line; the consistent package design makes cabinet looks streamlined rather than cluttered, just like in a luxury hotel. It also makes it easy for me to know when items need to be restocked. Incorporate these items into your guest bathroom to help your guests feel at home and comfortable:

Basic Items

☐ Bath towels	☐ New toothbrushes	☐ Makeup wipes
☐ Washcloths	☐ Toothpaste	☐ Razor
☐ Hand towels	☐ Mouth wash	☐ Hair dryer
☐ Shampoo & conditioner	☐ Deodorant	☐ Cotton swabs
☐ Hair spray	☐ Lotion	☐ Cotton balls

Luxury Items

☐ Facial oil	☐ Bath salts	☐ Manicure set
☐ Facial mask	☐ Loofah	☐ Scented candle

CHAPTER NINE

KID SPACES

I remember walking into the home of one client and feeling as though I had entered a daycare center. The feeling hit me as soon as I walked into an entryway that held a rack full of play costumes. The living room was almost devoid of furniture and was instead overflowing with toys. We eventually made it to the dining room; the table was covered in children's craft items and drawings were haphazardly taped to the walls. Even with the downstairs covered in kid's stuff, the children's bedrooms were still full of toys.

In almost every room in the home, the presence of children was felt—but the presence of adults was almost totally absent. This left the entire home feeling out-of-balance. As a guest in the home, I was actually uncomfortable because the space felt unwelcoming.

Many families make the mistake of giving up their space to accommodate their children, to one degree or another. It makes sense—after all, our children are members of our families. My job was to show this client that she could have a home where her kids are comfortable and welcome, and that her home could also be beautiful and welcoming for adults.

We began by dismantling the daycare. In truth, there were not enough hours in the day for the children to play with all the toys, so our first priority was to purge unnecessary items. I asked my client to fill a storage bin with toys; these could later be swapped out for the toys we were keeping in the house whenever the children became bored with their current selection.

I showed my client swatches of fabric and she began to get excited about the ways that she could make her home both beautiful and family-friendly. She chose a soft gray as a neutral, "adult" color that would complement a kid-friendly, happy shade of yellow. She chose comfortable furnishings—a sofa, chairs, and a large ottoman—for the entire family to enjoy. We included the kids in the decorating, asking them to paint abstract artwork for the space. We matted and framed the bright, cheerful pieces, and the kids were so proud to have their work on display.

As we worked through the rest of the house, our priority was to incorporate smart storage solutions for kid items. In the living room, we set up a play teepee in a beautiful gray-and-white striped fabric. It was darling in the space, and it immediately became a favorite place to play. It was also a place to quickly and easily store toys out-of-sight. We used inexpensive but attractive totes to store craft items, leaving the dining room table clear and ready for family mealtime. We removed the majority of toys from the children's bedrooms, although we did leave favorite stuffed animals and books. The bedrooms became peaceful retreats for each of the children.

In the end, my client—a busy mom of three—felt energized and empowered as she claimed and created balanced living spaces throughout her home.

◇

Children bring so much life to a home. However, they do have a way of generating clutter. Kids grow fast, which means they are always outgrowing toys, books, and clothing. Their things accumulate, and there's no avoiding that. However, it is possible to implement systems to manage kid "stuff" and to create a home that is comfortable and welcoming for *all* members of the family! The key is to understand how your children think and function so that they are able to contribute to keeping their things in order.

Of course, there are also many homes (like mine!) that are sans children. However, I do enjoy frequent visits from my nieces, nephews, friends with kids—and my grandchildren! As such, it's important to me that my home is kid-friendly.

STEP ONE: ASSESS KID SPACES

Although some spaces such as bedrooms and playrooms are dedicated to children, the other areas in your home are shared by the whole family and should be treated as such. As you consider your living room, kitchen, and other shared areas in your home, think about how the room is typically used by all members of the family and how you can incorporate kid-friendly elements without completely overwhelming the space. Remember, you want to avoid a "daycare" look!

STEP TWO: DECLUTTER KID SPACES

Whether you are attempting to organize a playroom, a child's bedroom, or another area in your home, the critical first step is to declutter. Although this task may seem daunting, it can actually be easier to purge kid items than adult items! Start by focusing on items that are broken, outgrown, or seldom-used.

◁ INVOLVE KIDS IN THE PROCESS ▷

Including your kids in on the decluttering process is a wonderful opportunity for you to teach skills for how to keep a neat and orderly space from a young age. As you work with kids in the decluttering process, it is important to talk with them to get their buy-in with purging items such as toys. Kids love to feel needed and helpful. Here are some ways to include and motivate your child:

Inspired Giving

Let your child know that the items they are giving up are going to a child in need. Sometimes kids are more willing to purge items if they think they are helping another child.

Make it a Game

Try playing a game of hoops with the decluttering bin. Play music and set a goal for the number of items your child should try to purge before the song is over. Get creative in ways to make decluttering feel less like work and more like fun!

Declutter Together

When I was a child, I remember the daunting task of cleaning my messy room by myself. It was miserable! I was always happy when a family member was willing to help, mostly because I enjoyed the time spent together.

Reward Your Child

Although you want to be careful not to create an expectation for tasks that you want your child to help with anyway, I do believe that children respond well to rewards. This could be as simple as a trip together to their favorite ice cream shop when the decluttering process is finished!

STEP THREE: *CLEAN KID SPACES*

I remember well the days of having to clean my disaster of a bedroom when I was a child. I would invite the neighborhood kids over to play and then let them leave without helping me to clean up. What was I thinking? More importantly, what did that mean for me? Typically, it meant that I would stuff everything under my bed and hope that my dad wouldn't look. (He always did!)

As we know, it is easier to clean a space when there is an easily identifiable place for everything. This is especially true for kids. There are a few other ways to motivate kids to help to keep their spaces neat:

◁ *DAILY ROUTINES* ▷

For kids, the trick is to make tidying their rooms a part of their daily routine. Many kids resist bedtime. Leverage your child's avoidance techniques to your advantage and allow "just five more minutes" *if* those five minutes can be spent putting toys, books, and other items in their proper places.

◁ *KID CLEANING CADDY* ▷

One way to involve your child in cleaning is to create a fun, kid-friendly cleaning caddy. Choose a caddy in a bright color and stock it with kid-safe items, like a brightly colored microfiber cleaning cloth.

◁ *THE CLEANING SONG* ▷

Good music can motivate me to clean! Create a children's cleaning playlist to make tidying time fly by!

STEP FOUR: *ORGANIZE* KID SPACES

I believe that kids need designated spaces for their items. Don't rush to buy new storage solutions just yet, though. Take the time to think about and understand how your child thinks, plays, and how they will be most likely to return their items when they are finished using them.

◁ *TOYS* ▷

Toys are important for many reasons, not the least of which is that they can be important to a child's development. Once you have decluttered toys to an appropriate number, begin to think about storage solutions. What you *don't* want is a toy box or bin that turns into a black hole for toys. Instead, you want items to be easy for your child to put away. Consider these types of storage solutions:

Under-bed Storage Bins

Under-bed storage bins pull double duty: they are great space savers and an ideal location for children to easily access their toys, and they also prevent children from being able to stuff items under their beds. Sort toys by like items into their respective rollaway bin under the bed. Label the bins so that your child can easily identify what is contained in each bin. If your child cannot yet read, you can utilize pictures to identify the items in each bin.

Totes

Totes are inexpensive and can be color-coded to easily identify items. If you have multiple children, you can even designate a certain color for each child. Totes are great because they are transportable; you can easily bring them from room to room, or even on a play date.

◁ CLOTHING STORAGE ▷

Kids constantly outgrow clothes and it can be a constant task to stay on top of their laundry! There are simple systems to help you—and your child—keep clothing items in order.

Closet and Dresser Storage

To keep kid clothes organized, I recommend creating complete outfits to hang in the closet or fold in a dresser drawer. This makes it easy for kids to get dressed each day, saving time in the mornings.

You may also choose to sort items by like kind or color. This keeps the closet or drawers looking neat and it makes it easy to identify clothing.

Small Items

For kid items that come in pairs such as socks and gloves, I recommend keeping a small bin in the closet to place mismatched or missing items. Hopefully, they will eventually reunite in this location.

Shoe Organization

The rule of thumb with shoe storage is to strive for simplicity. Shoe shelves in the bottom of your child's closet offer an accessible place to store shoes, rain boots, and the like. If your child is tall enough, you may also use a hanging shoe storage bag.

◁ CRAFT SUPPLIES ▷

Kids love to craft. (I can relate!) For kids and adults alike, crafting can quickly generate a mess. Implement easy-to-use systems to keep kid craft supplies in check. Create project bins to store paper, tools, stickers, and other items. Colorful stackable bins can also be a great solution. However, be sure that the bins aren't too heavy and don't stack them high.

◁ MONOGRAMMED TOWELS ▷

Monograms are a great way to personalize your children's bath towels. This is a wonderful way to make your child feel special and to encourage him or her to take ownership of their items. Simply buy the towels of your choice and take them to a local embroidery company. This is typically only a few dollars per towel.

STEP FIVE: *BEAUTIFY* KID SPACES

While kid spaces should be functional, they should also feel lively and happy, full of inspiration. There are a number of ways to achieve this with kid-friendly décor.

◁ COLOR ▷

Whether bold and bright or neutral and white, color plays an important part in kid spaces. Color can be very powerful; this makes choosing the colors in your child's space very important. Select colors that your child likes for his or her space to provide them with feelings of comfort and joy.

Kid items tend to come in a variety of vibrant colors. To keep things from becoming overwhelming, select just two or three colors that you can implement across the space.

It's also important to remember that kids' tastes can change. It may be easiest—and most cost-effective—to choose furniture and wall paint that are neutral and to bring in color through accessories like bedding and storage solutions like baskets and bins.

◁ ARTWORK ▷

The options for kid-friendly artwork are endless! You can follow the lead of my client from the beginning of this chapter and stylishly frame your child's artwork for display in your home. You can also search Etsy®, scour art shows, and browse your favorite retailers for artwork that will appeal to the kids in your life. Remember to look for pieces that complement the décor in your home while still being child-friendly.

◁ OTHER ACCESSORIES ▷

Rugs, throw pillows, blankets, and even lamps are all opportunities to add a playful yet chic vibe to your home. You can emphasize this more in kid-specific rooms like bedrooms and playrooms, and tone it down in spaces that are shared by the entire family. Remember to establish and stick to a limited color palette for a streamlined look that isn't over-the-top.

HOW A KID-FREE HOME CAN BE KID-FRIENDLY

Although we do not have any kids living in our home (minus our dogs, who are like our children!) I do like to create ways to entertain children when they visit. We love when family and friends bring children to our home; they are so inquisitive, fun, and full of energy that I wish I had! I have a few ways I prepare for their visits:

◁ MINI TOY BOXES ▷

One efficient way to create an instant kid-friendly space is to fill mini toy boxes. You can have boxes or bins for different age groups, each filled with items that appeal to that age. You might also choose to keep a separate bin filled with children's books.

I find that kids love the opportunity to play with things that are different from what they play with at home, so I intentionally stay away from toys that are popular today. Instead, I select toys that I grew up with, including pick-up sticks, Old Maid, and a Rubik's Cube®. Another fun idea is to create a "fort kit" with a bedsheet or blanket and clothespins stored in a bag. I promise that this simple idea offers hours of fun!

CHAPTER TEN

LAUNDRY ROOM
The MVP Space

There is no escaping laundry—it's truly a never-ending task. Many of us are forced to contend with the constant creep of laundry while working within space constraints. While this can be trying, I believe it's an invitation to get creative! This was especially true for one of my clients whose "laundry room" was a closet-sized space in the hallway of her home. She had previously tried to implement systems to organize this tiny space but became more frustrated with each failed attempt. The closet could fit only the washing machine and dryer with very little additional space to spare. While there was adequate space to fit an ironing board on the side wall, the bi-fold closet doors didn't offer any additional hidden storage opportunities.

My client's laundry closet was located at the very end of her hallway. As we assessed the space, I realized that the placement of the closet actually provided a way to "extend" the space out into the hallway, giving my client a larger area to work with. We began by installing a beautiful cabinet in the hallway, adjacent to the laundry closet. The piece of furniture gave a sense of grandeur to the hallway, but more importantly, it offered a place to cleverly store laundry supplies. A gorgeous lidded bowl atop the cabinet concealed laundry pods. A decorative lidded box held wool dryer balls, and the iron found its new home on an interior cabinet shelf. No one was aware that the beautifully styled cabinet concealed laundry supplies.

The final step in achieving laundry bliss was to eliminate the bulky plastic laundry baskets my client had accumulated. Instead, she incorporated attractive linen laundry bags with handles, storing the bags in different rooms throughout her home, easy to transport to the closet on laundry day. For this client, thinking creatively beyond her existing space was the key to achieving a functional laundry room!

The laundry room doesn't always get the respect it deserves. It is a hardworking space in every home, the room that helps us to keep our families and our homes tidy. It is also a space that means work. I am not a huge fan of doing laundry (is anyone?). In fact, laundry is probably my least favorite task, but oddly enough, my laundry room is one of the most beautiful, best-organized spaces in my house. This combination of beauty and function is a huge motivator for me when it comes to the tedious task of doing laundry.

STEP ONE: ASSESS YOUR LAUNDRY ROOM

Laundry rooms are considered utilitarian spaces, so we sometimes neglect to put forth the effort to organize them. However, because the laundry room plays such an essential role in helping us to maintain our homes, I believe it is worth the effort to transform the laundry room into an inviting space that reflects its importance in our daily lives.

Of course, a beautiful space stocked with the appropriate supplies is only half the battle. In fact, it means nothing at all if every surface is covered with piles of dirty laundry! I believe that the most important step to organizing your laundry room is to first address your laundry *routine*.

◁ ESTABLISH A SCHEDULE ▷

It is so important to have a weekly laundry schedule. One thing that I quickly learned as a young homemaker is that once you fall behind on laundry, it is *not* fun to play catch up. I liken the laundry process to a factory assembly line: all parts must keep moving to keep the flow. If any part of the process is delayed or stops, everything backs up and you soon have a disaster on your hands. A schedule encourages you to be as consistent with washing your laundry as you are with getting it dirty.

I know it sounds like a never-ending cycle. It is! But, laundry is still a task that can be relatively easily managed. It is about finding the system that works for you. We all have unique demands on our time, so the same laundry system may not work for everyone. Here are several laundry schedule options to help you discover what works best for you and your family.

Category Schedule

With the "category" schedule, a specific type of item is assigned to a certain day. For example, Monday might be the day that bedsheets and bath towels are washed; Tuesday might be the wash day for dad's clothing. This system works well if the members of your family each keep their own dirty clothes bin. It is straightforward to gather, wash, and put away items by their categories. However, if your family shares a centralized dirty laundry hamper, this system might not be the most efficient, as it would require you to sort dirty items into categories.

MONDAY . . . . > LINENS

TUESDAY . . . . > DAD'S CLOTHES

WEDNESDAY . . . . > MOM'S CLOTHES

THURSDAY . . . . > KIDS' CLOTHES

FRIDAY . . . . > MISCELLANEOUS

Laundry-by-Numbers Schedule

If you prefer to be less structured while still keeping up with laundry, the "laundry-by-numbers" system may work well for you. With this schedule, you commit to doing a certain number of loads of laundry per day. The laundry does not need to be categorized; you simply need to keep up with the number of loads and keep the process flowing. To make this schedule work, you must understand the number of loads you need to do each day in order to keep on top of the laundry. For an average family, try starting with one load for each day of the week. If the dirty laundry is still piling up, increase to two loads on two or three days. You will eventually determine the magic daily number of loads that your family requires.

Team-up Schedule

Laundry does not have to be an individual activity! I believe in sharing household responsibilities with the entire family. The "Team-up" schedule allows each family member to take on their preferred role in the laundry process. Here's how it works: each member of the family is responsible for one part of the laundry process. For example, I am responsible for putting clothes in the washing machine and dryer, and my husband is responsible for checking the dryer, folding, and putting away clothes. I do not enjoy the folding and putting away part of doing laundry, but my husband does not mind those tasks. On the other hand, my husband does not like to put clothes in the wash and to transfer them to the dryer. I love this system because once I have the clothes in the dryer, my job is done! The various stages of the laundry process can be adapted for the number of people in your family. For example, even young children are usually able to help put away clothes.

STEP TWO: *DECLUTTER* YOUR LAUNDRY ROOM

The laundry room can easily become a catch-all space for all manner of items, from pocket change to lost socks to outgrown clothing. As you declutter your laundry room, consider what truly belongs in this space. Are your cleaning supplies best kept here, or is it more functional to create mini-cleaning caddies that can be kept in their corresponding rooms? Can those extra towels be moved to the linen closet? Is that toolkit better kept in the garage? Remember that your goal is to keep only relevant items that serve a purpose in your laundry process!

STEP THREE: *CLEAN* YOUR LAUNDRY ROOM

As with other spaces that are used day-in and day-out, the laundry room benefits from routine daily tidying as well as periodic deep cleaning.

◁ DEEP CLEANING ▷

While it might seem odd to clean an appliance that is itself responsible for cleaning, it's actually quite important to keep your appliances working well! Read your washing machine owner manual to learn how (and how often) to disinfect your machine. This may be as simple as running a hot water cycle with bleach or vinegar. Likewise, familiarize yourself with your dryer owner's manual. What tips does it offer for maintaining your dryer? The manual may recommend cleaning the dryer hose at regular intervals—a task that is sometimes done by a professional, depending on your dryer setup.

After you declutter your laundry room, wipe down the shelves and mop or vacuum the floors. You may even wish to move your washer and dryer to vacuum and mop beneath the machines!

◁ DAILY CLEANING ▷

Dust bunnies tend to grow exponentially in the laundry room! Be sure to empty the dryer lint trap before you start a new load. Dust all the surfaces in the laundry room at least weekly. A damp microfiber cloth works well for gathering lint and the fine dust that commonly accumulates in laundry rooms.

STEP FOUR: *ORGANIZE* YOUR LAUNDRY ROOM

Without a doubt, laundry is the one thing in our homes that can get out of control in the blink of an eye. I am amazed by the amount of laundry that we accumulate in one week's time. Currently, two people and two dogs reside in our home; you would think that laundry would be an afterthought. Well, I am here to say that is *not* the case. In reality, you might think a football team lives with us based on the amount of laundry we produce in a week. If my small family generates this much laundry, I can only imagine what a family of four or more deals with on a weekly basis. Whether it serves a small or a big family—and whether the space itself is small or large—a laundry room should have specific tools to assist you with keeping on top of the wash.

UTILITY CLOSET ORGANIZATION

Utility closets hold essential tools that we need to care for our homes, such as brooms, vacuums, and overstock of home items like paper towels and cleaning supplies. Since this space often holds a wide variety of items, it is at high-risk to become cluttered.

The key to keeping a well-organized utility closet is to identify the exact items that will be stored in this space and establish appropriate storage for those items only, leaving no room for anything else.

I recommend dividing your utility closet into the following:

◁ CLEANING SUPPLIES ▷

Cleaning supplies are a necessity; they can be stored throughout the home for easy access. However, the utility closet is an ideal place for extra supplies, and for large supplies such as your vacuum and mop.

◁ VACUUM ACCESSORIES ▷

Many vacuums come with a variety of attachments. These can be very beneficial—but only if you can locate them when they are needed. I like to keep these accessories in a beautiful box on my utility closet shelf.

◁ TOOLS ▷

Although most tools will typically be stored in the garage, it can be handy to keep a mini toolkit inside your home, ideally in the utility closet, perfect for when you need a hammer to hang a piece of artwork or a screwdriver to change a battery in a device.

◁ BROOM, MOP, BUCKET, AND DUSTER ▷

The inside of your utility closet door offers excellent vertical storage, an ideal place to hang your broom, mop, and duster. Special hooks will prevent a landslide of items when you open your utility closet door! I love my collapsible mop bucket, an item that tucks away conveniently and saves so much space.

◁ CORDS ▷

Do you have to hunt for extension cords or spare phone chargers? Eliminate this frustration by keeping a "cord" bin in your utility closet. I like to put mini stackable organizers inside the box or bin so that I can categorize the cords.

◁ AROMATHERAPY ▷

I keep a little stash of candles and aromatherapy, consumable items that tend to get used quickly in my home. Create a space in your utility closet for these items. They will keep the space smelling fresh, and you will be able to easily see when your supply runs low.

◁ LAUNDRY STORAGE ▷

There are a variety of options for gathering and transporting laundry, from purely functional plastic laundry baskets to more decorative wicker hampers. The key is to find a basket, bag, or bin that works well in your home. My own system is simple: I store three laundry baskets on top of the cabinet in my laundry room where I can quickly grab one when taking the clean clothes out of the dryer. I love that these baskets have a permanent home in the laundry room so that they are always ready for use. My laundry room is small, so I use the available vertical space to store these baskets so that they do not take up valuable floor space.

In addition to these clean laundry baskets, each closet in my home holds a dirty clothes bag used to collect the dirty laundry that we wear throughout the week. These bags have handles and are therefore easy to transport to the laundry room, and it's simple to dump an entire load into the washing machine. I also prefer to not have clean clothes and dirty clothes sharing the same bins.

As you shop for laundry bins, think about your home and the type of bins that will be the most efficient for the space you have. Don't forget to consider vertical space in your laundry room or closets. Also, think about the style of the bins; select something that complements the decor of your laundry room, or something that will look beautiful in your closet.

◁ LAUNDRY SUPPLIES ▷

We definitely cannot do laundry without detergent, fabric softener, and dryer balls! These items can be bulky and unattractive, but there are creative ways to introduce appealing storage solutions. For example, I love to keep my laundry pods in pretty glass containers so that I can easily see when I am running low. While you don't necessarily have to be able to see these items, you do need to quickly access them. Properly labeled baskets or bins are an excellent way to store laundry-related items; just be sure to select containers that will accommodate the quantity you typically purchase.

In the age of bulk buying, it can be tempting to overstock your home with items. We think this will bring us convenience and efficiency; however, it typically only adds clutter—and in some cases waste if we do not use items by their expiration date. I prefer not to treat my home like a grocery store by overstocking products. Rather, I stock a reasonable supply of products for the size of my family and simply add items to my grocery list so that we do not run out of supplies. I won't pretend that I haven't attempted couponing or bulk buying. I most definitely have, but I quickly learned that the savings were not worth the time and space required. After all, stores almost

always have a "special" bargain, so I never feel pressure to stock up because I may miss out on saving a couple of dollars. It's more important to me to keep my home organized and free of unnecessary clutter.

◁ WALL STORAGE ▷

I often hang delicate items to air dry. For these items, I rely again on vertical space. We hung a retractable drying rack that uses minimal space in our small laundry room. I have also implemented wall storage solutions for my ironing board and iron, as well as for extra hanger space. These items are tucked neatly out of the way, but still easy to access when I need them. Even if your laundry room space is small, I encourage you to think creatively about the space you do have. For example, might you be able to use the back of the laundry room door for vertical storage?

◁ RANDOM ITEMS ▷

There are so many random items that are by-products of the laundry process: missing socks, loose change, lost buttons, bags for delicate clothing items, hangers to hang non-dryer items. The list goes on. It's important to set up a system to accommodate these random items in your laundry room so that it doesn't become a catch-all space. Begin by making a list of the miscellaneous items that typically come through your laundry room. Then, create a small area to accommodate these items. There are lots of options! You might hang a shoe door organizer on the back of your laundry room door or keep small makeup bags in a laundry room cabinet. As you know, I prefer to combine beauty and function, and so I marry my need for storage with my need for décor! I purchased nine miniature tin buckets for one dollar each and labeled each bucket with a category of random items; I then placed the buckets on decorative floating shelves. Anytime we have a missing button or need change, we know precisely where to go. For larger items, I incorporated bins on a different shelf: this is where I store mesh bags for delicate clothing and where we collect socks that are missing their mates. Eventually, the missing sock will turn up, though somehow there is always at least one sock that never finds its match!

STEP FIVE: *BEAUTIFY* YOUR LAUNDRY ROOM

Like many people, my laundry room is a space I spend time in each day. As with every area in my home, I want the room to feel special when I walk in. My laundry room features a beautiful chandelier, soothing gray walls, and a crisp white countertop.

I keep a lovely porcelain bowl on the countertop to collect dirty dish clothes until wash day. It's a room that I find soothing, despite the fact that it's associated with work (the fresh laundry smell doesn't hurt!). I encourage you to embrace the challenge to make your laundry room beautiful. Enjoy the positive energy your refreshed space will bring to your family life!

TIP

If you do your laundry outside of your home, I encourage you to create a mini laundry station, an easy-to-transport bag to hold your laundry essentials. Place detergent or laundry pods, dryer sheets or wool dryer balls, and any other items you require. This bag is ideal if you do your laundry in a laundromat or in an apartment laundry room, or for college students living in dorms. A mini laundry station is also useful in homes that have only a tiny laundry closet. When not being used, the mini laundry station can be stored under a bed or tucked inside a closet or bathroom cabinet. Hint: a backpack is great as it frees your hands to carry laundry.

HOW TO FOLD THE PERFECT TOWEL

At a young age, my mother taught me how to fold a towel beautifully to keep the linen closet neat and orderly with minimal effort. I have used this same technique throughout the years; it is my go-to fold for maintaining a beautifully organized linen closet. If we take the time to train ourselves to neatly fold towels (and other laundry items!), we reap the benefit with beautifully organized closet spaces throughout our homes. I want to share this simple, three-step folding technique, with thanks to my mother for teaching me this valuable tip when I was a little girl.

▶ STEP ONE To start, fold one end of the towel into the other end, cinching both corners together to fold the towel in half. Smooth the towel to remove any wrinkles.

▶ STEP TWO Next, fold the open end where the corners are held together into the closed fold of the towel.

▶ STEP THREE Last, turn the towel clockwise and fold the towel in by one third; repeat and fold in another third. Place the towel in your closet or cabinet with the closed end of the towel facing outward for a seamless, tidy look.

CHAPTER ELEVEN

SPECIALTY SPACES

With a little thought, it is possible to create spaces in your home to fuel your creativity, to foster personal growth, or to enhance your enjoyment of everyday life. One of my dear clients worked hard her entire life to care for her children and to provide a loving home for her family. She had recently retired and she was eager to dedicate a corner in her home for her creative pursuits.

My client had designated a walk-in closet as the area she wanted to use as her craft room, but she found that she wasn't using the space. We looked at the tiny area together, and I realized that although she had decided to use this space for crafting, she was still approaching it as a closet. The tiny room was filled with storage cube shelving, and all the crafting tools and supplies were in a bin on the very top shelf, making them difficult to access.

My job was to help my client to reimagine the area as her dream craft room. We completely emptied the room and painted it a bright white to give it an open feel. We installed a beautiful white crafting desk in the space, along with a comfortable, ergonomic chair. My client couldn't believe that the desk fit in the closet.

We used the vertical space and installed white shelving. On these shelves, we housed a variety of beautiful baskets to store craft items so that they were accessible. We brought the space to life with framed inspirational prints. In the end, this space was utterly transformed. My client instantly felt inspired, and she was overjoyed to have a space all her own.

Specialty spaces have become a staple in many houses. We all desire a fun place to pursue our interests, whatever they may be. These rooms can be beautiful additions and enhance the way you live. In my home, we created several specialty spaces by transforming rooms that were originally intended as bedrooms. My husband and I wanted our house to function well for us; multiple guest bedrooms did not feel like the best use of our real estate. We began a journey to figure out what specialty spaces would bring us the most joy.

This chapter explores a few types of specialty rooms and ways to approach these spaces to bring enjoyment. While not every one of my "steps" is included here, I have included the steps and tips that are most relevant to the space I am sharing with you. Many of these tips can be easily adapted to work in whatever type of specialty space is ideal for you and your lifestyle.

CRAFT ROOMS

◇

In the world of DIY, craft rooms are quite popular. People turn spare bedrooms, large closets, or even garages into craft spaces filled with things to help them express their creativity. Many people even start small businesses at home.

One pitfall of a craft room space is it can quickly become a disaster zone of materials used in the creative process. A craft room must have workable systems in place to function beautifully. You have to first understand how you will work in the space and then establish systems that will help you maintain order. After all, your craft room should be an enjoyable space rather than a source of frustration.

ASSESS THE SPACE

First, determine the purpose of your space. What type of crafts will you do in the area? Will this change over time? Is this your space for a specific kind of work, or will you do a variety of tasks? Will you run a business selling what you create? Once you establish the purpose of your room, you are ready for the planning phase.

When I started to put my craft room together, I rendered a simple room plan on a piece of paper. It was nothing fancy, but I worked out how I wanted the space to flow. I thought about where to place the craft table and where the cabinet and desk should be located. As you design your ideal craft room, I recommend that you first place the largest items in the space. Consider how you work so that you can organize and arrange the room to function in the way that best suits you.

Once you have placed the largest items in the space, it is time to think about where to place other elements. It was helpful for me to draw a rough diagram of the interior of each cabinet. As I created my "map," my goal was that anyone looking at the chart would be able to find anything I kept in the space. On your chart, document where you will store your items, down to the last crafting supplies and tools. Be sure to incorporate enough storage for your needs. Every item should have a home. Once you have completed your chart, get out the measuring tape to calculate the dimensions needed for storage.

DECLUTTER YOUR CRAFT MATERIALS

Before you attempt to organize your craft room space, first take time to declutter. You likely have a number of items that you do not (and will not ever) use. I recommend that you begin by following the decluttering process that I shared early in this book. Rid yourself of unused supplies and tools. If you struggle to let go of items, you might consider donating them to a teacher or to your church. Schools and churches are always in need of supplies and it can be easier to release your excess items when you know they will go to someone who can use them. Another idea is to divide items into little kits to donate to a local shelter for children.

I also encourage you to commit to "create in the present." I notice that creative people often collect items with the intent to work on future projects. They may fall victim to a great sale at a local craft store and load up on beads—beads that remain untouched for years. I have been guilty of this myself! When you declutter your craft room, keep only the things that you presently enjoy as a crafter. If you get bored with a specific type of craft, pass on your remaining supplies to someone who will appreciate and use them.

ORGANIZE YOUR CRAFT ROOM

You now know where everything will go, so it is simple to determine the size and type of organizers you will need for your space. I encourage you to think beyond traditional craft organization systems on the market as these can be quite pricey. You can find bins and baskets that function just as well for a fraction of the price.

Crafters all work differently. Some people love to set up craft rooms to be able to see all of their items; this stimulates their creativity. Others (such as myself) get overwhelmed by too much visual stimulation. I prefer for my craft materials to be concealed but easy to access. One approach is not better than the other, but you do need to figure out what motivates you to create!

◁ CRAFT TABLE ORGANIZATION ▷

The craft table is the main attraction of the craft room, just like the bed is the center of attention in a bedroom. If your bed is messy, the entire room looks messy. Have you ever seen a craft table covered with so much clutter that you wonder how they work in the space? Ideally, your craft table should remain relatively uncluttered to allow you to work effectively.

I recommend that you utilize one caddy on top of your craft table to hold all of your crafting tools. For my craft table, I selected tools that are the same color; this helps me to quickly identify items that belong, and it makes the area look pretty. If you have a small craft space, consider a craft table that offers storage in drawers or shelves under the table, allowing you to keep your tabletop clear.

◁ PEGBOARD ORGANIZERS ▷

Pegboards are a budget-friendly way to organize a variety of crafting items, ideal for people who prefer to see their things. Although I prefer to conceal most of my craft items, I do utilize a pegboard in the closet of my craft room. This allows me to simply close the door when I wish.

Pegboards can be beautifully styled to showcase your tools. However, a lot of thought goes into a well-functioning pegboard system. I recommend that you arrange the pegboard into categories; this is visually appealing and will help you quickly locate the item you need.

Don't forget to incorporate decorative elements into your pegboard to enhance the overall look. Choose items that provide both function and beauty, such as a small wall clock or a print with a motivational quote. Have fun and experiment with different looks! The great thing about a pegboard is that you can play around with the arrangement without putting holes in your wall.

◁ PROJECT BINS ▷

One thing I know is that creative people are not likely to work on just one project at a time. From a clutter perspective, this is dangerous as you will invariably create messes as you work on different projects. To manage this issue in my own craft space, I use project bins. These five simple bins allow me to store my projects and the associated materials individually. When I want to work on a project, I pull that specific bin and bring it to my craft table. This helps to keep my craft table free of unnecessary clutter and allows me to focus on one project at a time.

Have fun as you organize your crafting space; harness your creativity and use it to make a beautiful and fun area to spend time. Commit to a routine of tidying the area when you are done using it. Remember: if you take five minutes to put things away after you work, you won't have to spend hours cleaning later on.

BEAUTIFY YOUR CRAFT ROOM

I believe that we draw inspiration from the spaces around us. It makes sense to take time to make your craft room beautiful so that when you withdraw to this space, your creativity will be sparked by your surroundings!

Excellent lighting is very important in a craft room. In addition to overhead lights, look for attractive task lamps to help you highlight whatever project you may be working on.

Consider other elements that get you into your creative "zone." If you like to listen to music as you work, put a small speaker in your craft room. What colors inspire you? Look for opportunities to incorporate these colors into your storage solutions, wall art, or even your crafting tools. Your craft room is all about finding ways to express yourself creatively. Embrace this notion in your approach to decorating the space, too!

MEDIA ROOM

Media rooms (also called theater rooms) are also popular specialty spaces in many modern homes. Talk about a fun area! A media room is a great place for a family to spend time together and enjoy a night at home. With today's technology, there are many ways to create a space that offers an enjoyable experience for family and guests.

A few years ago, my husband and I decided that we wanted to create a theater room in our home. The only possible location was in our smallest spare bedroom. We immediately started to plan how we could make this space our home theater. It was a lot easier than we thought, and it is one of the most used areas in our home on the weekends.

ASSESS YOUR MEDIA ROOM

When we began to dream of our media room, we knew that we wanted to give our guests (and ourselves!) an enjoyable, theater-like experience. I love the authentic feel of a traditional theater in the coziness of home. In the process of creating our media room, I embraced this concept as we designed and organized the space. For example, a platform that provides "raised" seating is a great addition to any theater room. A premade platform can be purchased, or it can be built by anyone with basic woodworking abilities.

Proper theater seating can cost a pretty penny. However, when you create a theater at home, you can be creative when choosing your seating and still achieve the look of a traditional theater.

As you select seating, think about how many people you will typically have in the space. It's also important to think about comfort. Do the seats recline? Where will drinks go? Where will technology controllers be stored? You want this space to function well, so take the time to think through these details. In our theater room, I opted for simple recliners that complement the style of my home. The recliners are comfortable and not too bulky, perfect for the small space we have.

ORGANIZE YOUR MEDIA ROOM

Organizing a theater or media room can be fairly straightforward. Of course, a media room needs a beverage and snack center. You also want to plan for ways to store DVDs, games and accessories, and any other items to enhance your space.

◁ BEVERAGE AND SNACK CENTER ▷

Half the fun of a movie is popcorn and a beverage! Stock food and drinks in quantities that are appropriate for your family size or the number of guests you will entertain in the space. You can incorporate a mini fridge, popcorn machine, and candy bar. My husband and I transformed the closet in our media room into a snack bar. We built a huge box that slid into the closet, and then incorporated cabinets and counters into the box. We chose not to build directly into the closet so that if we ever decide to sell our home, we can easily convert the space back into a bedroom.

Create a Candy Bar

The candy bar in our media room is dangerously tempting, but I love it. You do not need an elaborate set-up; your candy bar can be as simple as a drawer. Be sure to select favorite family treats. In my candy drawer, I offer delicious luxury chocolate and candy for my guests, a little something out of the ordinary. I also like to stock a few savory items.

Be sure that the candy won't melt where you store it. For example, it's not a good idea to store candy near a heating vent. Organize the candy by like items; this will help you easily determine when you need to restock.

Beverage Fridge

It's so nice to have a beverage fridge in the media room; we have certainly gotten our money's worth from ours. I recommend that you limit this fridge to beverages only. Include a variety of options for your family and friends. It's a nice touch to place drinking glasses on one shelf in the fridge; family and guests can always have a nice, chilled glass for their beverages.

◁ *GAMING ORGANIZATION* ▷

Although we do not have young children at home, our adult children used to love their gaming consoles. Gaming is a big part of many households; it's useful to have a simple and efficient way to organize games and gaming accessories. It can take very little for gaming systems to take over a space. As you organize your media space, try to conceal as much of the technology as possible. For example, you may be able to mount gaming systems and consoles behind the television. The less you can see the better. This will take a little planning and effort initially, but the payoff is enormous. Another way to minimize clutter is to store game discs in small binders.

BEAUTIFY YOUR MEDIA ROOM

There are a variety of ways to make your theater room a cozy, beautiful space in your home. If the room has large windows, consider installing attractive blackout blinds or drapes. These will enhance the room's décor and help to block light when it's movie time.

> **TIP**
>
> Paint your media room walls with a dark color for a cinema feel and to prevent light from reflecting onto the television screen.

If you are a movie buff, you may think about featuring framed movie posters of your favorite films. Or, consider framed prints with your favorite movie lines!

Think of adding cozy throw blankets to your media room; these can add a burst of color and will be appreciated by your guests—especially if you are showing a scary film!

Remember, this room is meant to be fun! There are all sorts of ways the décor of your theater room can reflect your personality, so get creative!

◇

Whatever your hobbies, I encourage you to imagine ways to make your home fit your lifestyle. Don't get stuck in a rut thinking that you have to keep a bedroom a bedroom, or that you cannot have a home gym or spa because your house is too small. With a little effort, a house of any size can become your dream home!

CHAPTER TWELVE

GARAGE
The Commuting Space

I remember the reaction that I received from a client when I informed him that the first step in the process of organizing is garage would be to remove every single item from the space. If looks could kill, I would not be here to write this book. This client's garage was filled to the limit with tools, mowers, box after box, and many other random items. It was a storage facility. There wasn't walking room, so there certainly wasn't enough space to park a car.

From the outset, my client was highly resistant to the idea of decluttering. The last thing I wanted to do was waste time struggling to convince him to purge items. I took a different approach: I chose to visually motivate my client by showing him a completely clean space—a clean slate, so to speak. We began by renting a U-Haul to temporarily house all the items from the garage. With the space cleared and cleaned, I arranged to have a beautiful, durable garage floor installed. I brought in cabinets specially made for garage storage. It was beautiful—and empty! The look of happiness on my client's face was priceless. This was the garage of his dreams.

With the perfect garage right in front of him, my client was suddenly determined to declutter. Before we brought any items back into the space, we walked around the garage together with a pad of sticky notes; we put a note on each shelf, cabinet drawer, and area to identify what should go where. My client designated an area for tools, one for lawn equipment, and another for storing holiday decorations. Most importantly, he now had a place for his car! Once the areas were defined, my client was a rock star—he brought only the items he truly needed back into the garage. Best of all, since the remaining items were still in the U-Haul, it was easy to drive them to the donation center. For this client, the key to success was actually flipping my tried-and-true process on its head, and the end result was a beautifully organized garage!

———————◇———————

If you walked into your garage right now, what would you encounter? Is your vehicle parked in the garage? Would you trip over roller blades or piles of recycling? If you were given thirty second to locate a tape measure, would you be able to find it?

While organizing the garage—the catchall space for many families—may feel like a daunting task, it's not a reality that is out-of-reach. Can you imagine pulling your car into a tidy, shiny garage when you arrive home each evening? This dream can come true with some elbow grease, careful planning, and with the implementation of smart organization systems.

STEP ONE: *ASSESS* YOUR GARAGE

As you consider your garage, think about how the space can best serve you and your family. The first and most obvious question to ask yourself is whether you intend to park a vehicle (or two) in your garage. The garage is often also used for storage, as a workshop, or as an informal entry into the house. I have even seen a garage used as an extended game room, home to a ping pong table!

STEP TWO: *DECLUTTER* YOUR GARAGE

Perhaps more than any other space, the garage has the potential to collect years' worth of clutter. It's not a part of the main living space, so the garage can become an easy drop zone for all kinds of items that don't have an obvious place within the home: sports equipment, tools, seasonal décor, and so on.

While items that you actually use throughout the year are often stored in the garage, it's the items you *don't* use that really cause trouble. Often, these items are out-of-sight, out-of-mind. Have you ever moved furniture or unused exercise equipment to the garage to free up room in your house? If you have children, you know that they quickly outgrow sports equipment, bicycles, and toys. Perhaps your garage is home to items like these.

My husband and I have fallen into this trap, too. We used to keep a variety of gardening tools in our garage: shovels, rakes, hoes, and other specialty tools. They were well-organized on wall-mounted racks. However, over time we began to pay for someone to maintain our yard. When we made this change, we were able to give away most of our large yard maintenance tools, keeping only the essentials.

As you declutter your garage, honestly assess the things you store in the space. Don't hold on to items if you have no reason to use them.

STEP THREE: *CLEAN* YOUR GARAGE

Dust, leaves, and grass clippings have a way of blowing into even the tidiest of garages. If you are attempting to organize your garage after a long period of neglect, you may want to follow the lead of the client I told you about at the beginning of this chapter and remove all of the items from the space. Then, when you can proceed without tripping over stray items, you will be able to sweep and dust until your garage sparkles.

STEP FOUR: *ORGANIZE YOUR GARAGE*

The garage is an ideal storage zone simply because it's often a large space. Even if you park vehicles in your garage, there is usually space around the perimeter of the garage (or even in the rafters!) for shelving and storage. The key is to keep the storage space streamlined and well-organized. The simplest way to keep your garage in order is to make everything easy to access. When you need a tool or a nail, you should be able to quickly locate and grab what you need so you can get on with your project. Of course, the first step is to establish systems that support your organization needs. The second step is to commit to putting away items when you have finished with them.

◁ GARAGE CABINETS AND WORKSPACE ▷

Installing garage cabinets can be expensive, but it's a worthy investment to help you keep order in your garage. Cabinets offer ample, flexible storage for a variety of items. Along with cabinets, we installed a coordinating work table in our garage to provide my husband with woodworking space.

◁ VERTICAL SPACE STORAGE SOLUTIONS ▷

Mounted ceiling racks from companies such as SafeRacks.com® are smart storage solutions. You can store infrequently used items—such as holiday décor—in bins without taking over shelf or cabinet space in the garage.

Wall shelves are also ideal, easy-to-install organizing solutions. They are affordable and a great way to utilize vertical space. I store tool boxes that hold random garage items on the shelves in our garage.

◁ TOOL ORGANIZATION ▷

The garage is an ideal place to house tools that help to maintain the home, from traditional repair or carpentry tools to gardening tools. Some items can be unwieldy and take a lot of space, like a lawn mower. Other items can best be stored by maximizing vertical wall space, such as shovels and rakes. In the previous chapter, I discussed pegboards as an ideal wall storage solution in a craft room. Pegboards are also fabulous storage solutions in a garage! A pegboard allows you to visibly store tools in together in one space.

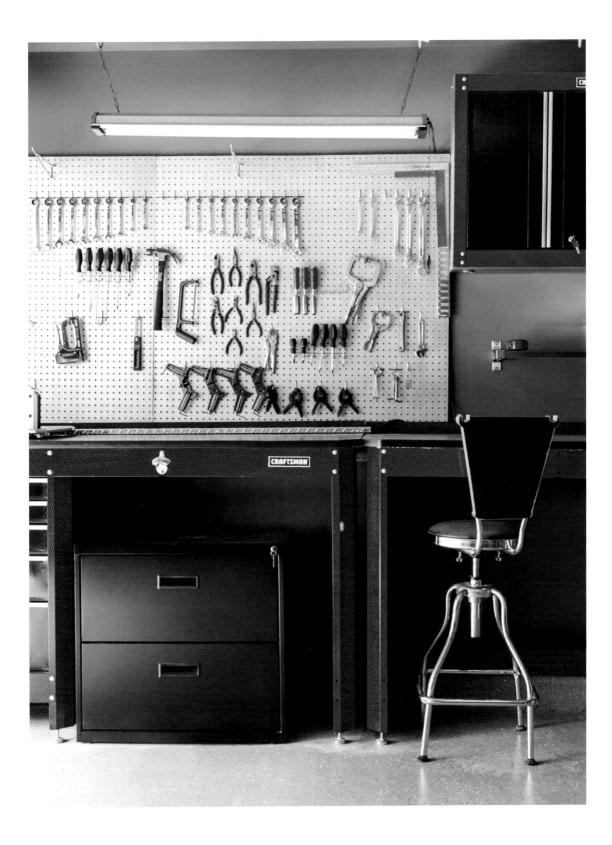

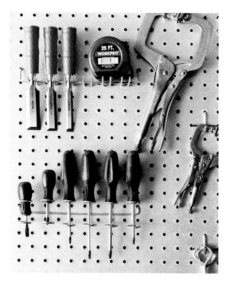

Toolboxes are compact, handy organizers for the garage space. My husband has a huge collection of tools. Many are special to him because he has collected them over the years. He worked as a mechanic as a young man, and he still holds the mechanic's perspective that tools get better with age. (To me, this means more clutter!) To keep his tools in order, we use a large toolbox on wheels. It is big enough to accommodate all his tools, and it can be easily moved and used in different areas.

◁ GARDENING CENTER ▷

I probably will never win any gardening awards, but I still love to work in my garden. I keep our lawn and garden supplies stored so they are easy to access and protected through the seasons. I use large plastic bins to categorize and store soil, fertilizer, grass seeds, and pest control products. The bins are narrow and stackable, so they save a great deal of space and look neat and orderly. Our gardening tools are neatly and conveniently stored on wall-mounted racks.

◁ RECYCLING CENTER ▷

I recommend keeping a home recycling center in the garage. You don't want to store empty containers and old newspapers inside your home. I use simple, open bins to sort recyclable items like cans, glass, plastic, and paper. I also recommend that you keep a "donate" bin where you can collect items you no longer need. If your garage is small, you can use stackable bins to save space.

◁ *PAINT AND HOME DÉCOR ITEMS* ▷

As you maintain and update your home, you will often have extra paint, flooring remnants, and other DIY leftovers. It can be helpful to keep these items in case you need to do a paint touch-up or even replace a floorboard or tile. (Just make sure you retain only the samples that are relevant for your current décor!)

TIP

To keep track of the name and color code for the paint in a room, note the details on the inside of a light switch plate using a Sharpie® marker. You will always know where to find the paint details for touch-ups.

An efficient (and attractive) way to store leftover paint is in mason jars. The jars take less space than paint cans and it is easy to identify paint colors. I recommend that you remove the paint color code from the can and secure it to the lid of the jar or create a new label entirely.

Organize spray paint by color to make it easy to identify the paint you already have on hand (and prevent you from wasting money on new cans).

◁ *HOME MAINTENANCE ITEMS AND "RANDOMS"* ▷

There are many random items required to keep your home in order: light bulbs, paint brushes, duct tape, and so much more. I like to organize these items by category and store them in labeled tool boxes to keep my garage organization streamlined (and even stylish!).

For random automobile and home maintenance products like car cleaning supplies, paint remover, or caulk, I try to categorize items just as my local hardware store does. Again, store like items together on a shelf or in a cabinet so they are easy to find when you need them.

STEP FIVE: *BEAUTIFY YOUR GARAGE*

You may be asking yourself, "What do I care if my garage is *beautiful?*" Trust me—you may not believe it's necessary, but I guarantee you will enjoy the space if you put forth the effort to make it visually appealing!

Think about your garage space from the ground up. What does the floor look like? Is there dirty or stained concrete underfoot? Consider installing interlocking tiles made specifically for garages or painting the garage floor with durable epoxy paint for a finished look.

Garage cabinets and storage solutions can often be customized and configured to fit your space. Again, this can be an investment, but one that will absolutely pay off in the long run in terms of your ability to keep the space organized and user-friendly. (Some of these cabinets even come in fun, bright colors!)

Also consider lighting. Is your garage lit by a single dinky light bulb? Adequate lighting is useful if you plan to work on projects in your garage; bright lights also provide a cheerful welcome home when you pull your car into the garage at night.

CAR ORGANIZATION

It should be fairly simple to keep the car organized, yet many people struggle to do so. Often, people treat their automobiles almost as an extension of their home; this almost always leads to clutter in the car. Further, trash tends to accumulate in cars. There is no built-in trash can, and therefore no logical place to dispose of receipts, straw wrappers, and empty beverage containers.

Begin to think of your vehicle as something that exists to transport you from one point to another. With this view, you might not feel the need to keep as many items in your car. Your vehicle should be clean, beautiful, and organized to support your lifestyle.

◁ *THE GLOVEBOX* ▷

The glovebox is a magnet for car clutter. Avoid the urge to cram it with items simply because you can close it off. Rather, the glovebox is the perfect place to store essential items. Use this space to store driving documents (registration and proof of insurance), the driver's manual, and a contact book that lists important contact information. I keep a physical list of my family's mobile and work phone number in my glovebox just

in case my mobile phone battery is dead and I need to make a call. I also like to keep a notepad and pen in the glovebox in case I need to leave a note for someone.

◁ CENTER CONSOLE ▷

In my center car console, I keep a little black bag filled with hand wipes and hand sanitizer for eating on the go. I also store a long mobile phone charger that reaches from the front to the back seat. Finally, I keep a microfiber cloth in the console to quickly wipe away dust in my car.

◁ DOOR POCKETS ▷

The driver's side door pocket is a perfect place to store an umbrella, along with a mini trash bin to keep the car tidy. I also keep a larger compact garbage can in the passenger door pocket for long trips.

◁ TRUNK ▷

Try to keep your trunk space empty so that you have room to fit groceries and other items. If you have children who are involved in activities, you might consider using a trunk organizer to hold any sports equipment they use daily. You will prefer this to a soccer ball rolling around the back of your car!

CHAPTER THIRTEEN

PET ORGANIZATION

H aving a pet does not mean that you have to sacrifice having a beautiful home. Our pets add so much to our lives. Their things can and should be beautifully organized in your home to conveniently maintain all that you need to care for them. Consider your home aesthetic as you incorporate pet items into your spaces. Store these items near where they will typically be used.

◁ PET TOYS ▷

Pets love their toys, and they provide them so much happiness (and give you a little break from playing catch all day). When shopping for toys for Bentley and Albert, my two little Yorkies, I consider both function and style. Their favorite toys are balls and toys with tails. From a functional perspective, I specifically look for these types of toys. From a style perspective, I make sure to get the toy in colors that match my home decor. When my dogs spread their toys throughout the living room, the space doesn't appear to be cluttered because the toys actually comple-ment the space! I can also leave their toys in a beautiful little basket in my living room, and it blends right into the area. Now, of course, you are going to always find that one shiny toy that you must get for your pet. I say go for it! It is all about making them happy.

◁ PET FOOD ▷

The size of your pet and your pet's type of food will dictate the kind of food stor-age solution you require. Food for smaller pets tends to come in smaller quantities, making it easier to store. Because I have small dogs, I use a beautiful white porcelain canister personalized with their names. I place the canister on the fireplace mantle in my kitchen, close to their bowl. When storing pet food, you do not need to resign yourself to an unattractive plastic tub or big bags of dog food in your pantry. Yes, either of these options may be functional, but they detract from the beauty of the space. In reality, you can have the best of both worlds! There are many beautiful pet food containers for small and large animals alike. If you prepare pet food and store it in your refrigerator, you can buy a container in a specific color to make the pet food easily identifiable.

When it comes to pet bowls, I recommend keeping it simple. A traditional pet bowl comes in silver and blends in with many home styles. There are many other pet bowl options: rose gold, gold, white, black, and all the colors of the rainbow. It is relatively easy to find a pet bowl to coordinate with your home décor.

◁ PET BEDS ▷

One of my favorite things to buy for my Yorkies are beautiful beds. In every space in my home where there is seating, I am sure to include a bed for my pets. They are family members and I incorporate their needs throughout the home just as I do for my other family members. When shopping for pet furniture, I adopt the same mindset as I do when shopping for normal furniture: I consider comfort, color, and size.

There are so many excellent retailers that offer pet bedding to complement your home. You may even DIY a pet bed to fit your style! My husband created the pet bed on our patio. He built a simple wooden box, and I purchased a home decor pillow that coordinated with our decor. Our dogs love this bed. There are many online tutorials that offer step-by-step instructions to create a beautiful dog bed. If DIY is not your cup of tea, you can always get someone to make a custom piece of pet furniture. It is definitely worth the effort, both for your pet and for the beauty of your home.

◁ *PET SUPPLIES* ▷

Pets often have a variety of accessories to accommodate their needs: leashes, hygiene products, and medicines. These items can create a lot of clutter in your home if you do not have a dedicated space for them. It can be frustrating to keep up with pet items if you do not have an organized system in place. To accommodate pet supplies, you should designate a space exclusively for these items. This may be a drawer in your entryway or a bin in your coat closet. The key to success is to organize pet supplies in the location where they are frequently used. For example, if you walk your dog every day, you may want to organize pet things in an area close to the front door, as opposed to an upstairs closet. I like to organize pet supplies by category:

▶ ACTIVITIES Leashes and on-the-go/travel items
▶ HYGIENE Bathing items, wipes, towels
▶ MEDICAL Pet medications

I also like to place certain pet items in smaller bags, making them easy to transport as needed. For example, it is faster to pull pet bathing items from the drawer if these items are organized into one smaller bag.

◁ PET BINDER ▷

Your pet deserves to have a file with all of their relevant documents, just like every other member of your family. This makes it convenient for veterinary appointments, when you travel with your pet, and at other times during your pet's life. Take your pet binder with you when you travel in case your pet needs medical care. If you do not want to transport a binder, you can always save an electronic copy that you can access on the go. Your binder should include the following information:

General Pet Information

This includes your pet's name, date of birth, breed, color, any identifying marks, favorite food, favorite toy, feeding times, the kind of food that they eat, and habits. It is important to document this information so that you can easily provide it to pet caregivers as needed.

Pet Photo

It is important to have a pet photo in case your pet gets lost. In addition to keeping your pet's photo in their file, you should also include your pet's photo in your emergency preparedness binder, which I discuss in chapter six.

Proof of Ownership

Just like you have a birth certificate for your children, you want to have ownership paperwork for your pet.

Spare Identification Tags

I like to keep an additional pet tag with our information engraved in our pet file in case an existing tag is lost or damaged.

Veterinary Records

It is also important to keep pet medical history records on file. It is critical to be able to provide the significant medical history for your pet if necessary. You may also require this information for pet insurance reimbursement purposes.

Vaccine Records

Keep your pet's current vaccine records on file. You may need to access these records for a variety of reasons, including kenneling your pet, training, or in the event of an incident. Also include your pet's rabies certificate on file as proof that your pet is up-to-date on this important vaccination.

Pet Insurance

Pet insurance can be a money-saving investment when it comes to caring for your pet. If you decide to get pet insurance, be sure to maintain all the relevant information as it pertains to claims and payments.

Legal Trust

As with any other family member, in the event of your death, you want to make sure that your pet is cared for. Having a trust can provide you with a peace of mind that your pet will be cared for.

Emergency Numbers

List numbers that relate to your pet, such as your emergency veterinarian and pet poison hotline.

CONCLUSION

My goal with this book is to inspire you to think of home organization not as a task, but as a wonderful opportunity to cultivate a beautiful environment and wonderful experiences for anyone who enters your home. Simply put, I want you to fall in love with your home.

Removing clutter from your home and life has such an impact in helping you to achieve a stress-free and happy life. Accomplishing—even *starting*—to declutter and organize your home is a big undertaking. Keep in mind, though, that once you find your way to an organized space and devote the thought and time to making your home beautiful and welcoming, you will eventually be able to devote less time to big messes and will instead be able to focus on enjoying your home and your life, with less overall time necessary to keeping your space tidy.

Of course, this is a process. You are not alone on your journey to bring organization and tranquility into your home and life. I am honored that this book is your companion as you approach your space. By following the simple steps through each space, one space at a time, your motivation and inspiration will grow as you beautifully organize your home.

Your home is a personal expression of *you*. Whatever your stage of life—whether you are a stay-at home parent, a working professional, or retired—you should strive for your best life. Especially at home.

INDEX